Wicked

ADIRONDACKS

Dennis Webster

THE
History
PRESS

Published by The History Press
Charleston, SC 29403
www.historypress.net

Copyright © 2013 by Dennis Webster
All rights reserved

First published 2013

Manufactured in the United States

ISBN 978.1.60949.717.0

Library of Congress CIP data applied for.

This book is dedicated to the people who live within the blue line of the Adirondack Mountains. These hearty residents reside under the shade of tall pines while fighting the bloodsucking black fly horde, and for that, they are truly noble. I'd also like to dedicate this book to my longtime first reader and cousin Evelyn Webster, whose positive feedback and expert guidance helped make this book possible.

Contents

Preface

I have spent my life fascinated by the grandeur of the Adirondack Mountains, the most unique mountain range on the planet Earth. The Adirondacks have an abundance of water. Lakes, rivers, streams and ponds are strewn throughout the range. The glaciers of the Ice Age pushed up the rocks that make up the Adirondack Mountains and then melted and retreated, leaving behind the aqua-laced beauty before us. I have climbed the fire tower of Rondaxe Mountain, fished the lake trout of Piseco Lake, walked the shops of Old Forge and slid down the bobsled run on a luge sled on Mount Van Hoevenberg in Lake Placid. The area within the "blue line" is the most marvelous I have ever encountered in all my travels. It's within the grandeur of the Adirondack Mountains, below the needles of the tall pines, that the criminal activities and insidious events detailed in this book occurred, and by no means are they an indication of the noble and honest residents who make this beautiful area their home. I handpicked the following stories as I scoured through historical archives. I always tell readers that I pull out stories I find fascinating, did not know or thought would be of interest to the readers. Now, let's pull up one of those random Adirondack Mountain boulders and examine the criminal crawly things that squirm underneath.

Acknowledgements

I would like to thank editors Whitney Tarella and Darcy Mahan and the staff at The History Press for giving this book a home. Writers cannot exist in a vacuum and must rely on friends to give them advice, assistance and a shoulder to cry on. I would like to thank Bernadette Peck, the website Murderpedia.org, Caryl Hopson, Susan Perkins, Woody Sins, the Herkimer County Historical Society and the Fulton County History website. I'd also like to thank my mother and father, Milton Lee and Charlene Webster, as well as my wife, Kelly Webster, and my children, Ashley, Jakob and Stephanie, for their patience, understanding and love.

Introduction

The Adirondack Mountains

The Adirondack Mountains are part of the Adirondack Park system and are considered a new mountain range made up of old rocks that had been pushed up into the beautiful dome of forty-six peaks at an elevation over four thousand feet. There are over 2,500 rivers, lakes, ponds and streams within the eighteen thousand square miles that make up the Adirondacks. The uniqueness of the Adirondack Mountains is in the sheer amount and styles of water upon them. Melting glaciers left waterways strewn in awe-inspiring amounts that exist nowhere else on this spinning ball of mud. The Adirondack Mountains are located in the northeastern part of New York State and include Clinton, Essex, Franklin, Fulton, Hamilton, Herkimer, Lewis, Saint Lawrence, Saratoga, Warren and Washington Counties. The Adirondack Park boundary contains the entire Adirondack Mountain range and is called the "blue line." Lake Champlain and Lake George border the eastern side of the range. The Mohawk Valley borders the south, and the Tug Hill Plateau is to the west. The name Adirondack is a version of the Mohawk *ratirontaks*, meaning "they eat trees," a moniker given to Algonquian-speaking tribes located in the mountains who were said, when food was scarce, to eat the buds and bark of trees. The Adirondack Mountains are a popular tourist attraction that bring in admirers from all over the world coming to climb the peaks, boat on the lakes, fish in the ponds, white-water raft on the rivers, jump down the water slides of Water Safari and walk the hallowed ground of Olympic champions at Lake Placid. It's within this range that guides stomped and crime simmered between the pines and along the banks of the liquid nights. It's with this love and devotion to the glorious Adirondack Mountains that I present to you a taste of the evil side of the beauty, the criminal side, the side that fascinates and brings forth fear—fear beneath the shadows of the steep cliffs of the Adirondack Mountains.

Chapter 1

Nat Foster, Indian Killer

"Ha. Nat Foster, you bad man, you kill Indians."
—Indian Hess, on meeting legendary woodsman and trapper Nat Foster

Disclaimer: The following account was taken almost exclusively from the book *The Life and Adventures of Nat Foster, Trapper and Hunter of the Adirondacks* by A.L. Byron-Curtiss. Although Nat Foster is well known as a legendary hunter, trapper and woodsman, most of his tales come from this single book, based almost entirely on verbal legends and some interviews with Nat's descendants. The book was published in 1897, and the language, especially with regard to Native Americans, is of the time period—thus the phrasing "Indians" and "Injuns." Never in Byron-Curtiss's book did I find any particular tribe mentioned. It's always "Indians." I found it peculiar that Nat's father, Nathanial Foster, had fought bravely in the Revolutionary War and used his interactions with the Native Americans at that time to build a hatred of that race that he would ingrain into his children, especially Nat. Nathanial fought at the Battle of Oriskany, where it is well known that the Oneidas fought bravely to help this country gain its freedom from Britain. However, Nathanial makes no mention of this bravery or the fact that the Oneidas died to help the colonists. The Oneidas' decision to assist the colonists broke apart the Iroquois alliance, as the other tribes would fight alongside the Loyalists. What I'm describing in the following account takes us back to another time, a time when a man would be judged on the color of his skin or be slandered based on the actions of some who might not even had been affiliated with his tribe. With this disclaimer out of the way, I give you the tale of Nat Foster, Indian killer.

BEGINNING OF AN INDIAN KILLER

The woodsman Nat Foster was well known in the southern Adirondacks as a man who could load and fire his flintlock quicker than any man known to carry the weapon. In the rugged eighteenth century, the Adirondacks was a place where wild animals roamed and only the heartiest of humans could hunt, live and survive. Nat Foster was certainly one of the best-known woodsmen, but he had a side to him that we in the modern age could say was rather brutal. However, we have to go back to the time and place of his life and determine what exactly led Nat Foster to kill his fellow man, making him famous as an Indian killer.

It all started when Nathanial Foster was born in a solitary log cabin in the rugged backwoods of Hinsdale, New Hampshire, on June 30, 1764. His father's name was also Nathanial, but everyone called his son Nat. Young Nat's father was an accomplished man with his knife and his guns. Nat learned sharpshooting and survival skills from his father, as well as from Nat's older brother, Elisha, known as "Lish," who was only a few years older than Nat. At the time, the Fosters had seven children, and all of them were brought up to hate and distrust Indians. Nat's father had encountered Native Americans before and during the Revolutionary War. The Loyalists had started to ply Native Americans with rum, animal skins and other goods to push them to lash out against colonists in order to drive them out or force their loyalty to the British. Nat Foster's father would say that Indians were his greatest enemy and that they would steal supplies, burn down settlements and scalp colonists under the guide of their Loyalist employers.

One Loyalist in New Hampshire was William Wilson, a stamp agent who lived a life of wealth with his wife and daughters, all the while paying off Indians to commit deeds against settlers. After the Foster family lost all of their livestock to what they thought were Indians, Nathanial Foster swore he'd shoot all Indians. During a meeting on the Revolution, seven-year-old Nat stood up and told the assembled men and his father when they were discussing going to Boston to fight the British, "Yes, Dad, you go, and Lish and me'll stay home and shoot Injins."

REVOLUTIONARY WAR

Nathanial Foster would leave his family and head off to fight in the Revolutionary War, where he would fight at Concord and Bunker Hill and serve next to George Washington, in addition to fighting at the Battle of Oriskany and the Battle of Saratoga. This father would turn down promotions in order to keep a musket in his hand instead of an officer's sword. His absence would force young Nat and Lish to grow up quickly and be the men of the house, even though they were still young boys. Nathanial Foster would nurture his hatred of Indians with the scalpings he witnessed during the war, yet there is no mention of what he thought of the brave

Nat Foster and his older brother, Lish. *A.L. Byron-Curtiss.*

Oneida Indians who fought on the side of the colonists at the Battle of Oriskany against the British. The Oneidas would break the strong bond of their Native American Iroquois brotherhood in order to help the colonies secure their freedom.

There were many cases of Native Americans assisting colonists and working to secure safety in the rugged frontier, but Nathanial seemed unmoved by these gestures of goodwill, stating to his Revolutionary comrades, "Boys, I've seen enough of their fiendishness in our excursions up the Mohawk Valley to make me and my children enemies." He would pass this hatred onto his children where their folkways and mores would be paid in Indian blood. He saw a cabin burned to the ground and a mother and her young children murdered and assumed that Indians had done it. Nathanial Foster did blame the British for the actions of the rogue Indians, stating that the redcoats "are more despised then [*sic*] the Indians themselves."

Although Nathanial Foster was a war hero and big contributor to the freedom of the colonists from the British, he couldn't get beyond his blinding hatred for an entire race of human beings and passed this viewpoint onto his children, especially young Nat. Nathanial told everyone who would listen that he would "teach my children to fear god but not the copper face of an Injun." Nat Foster would adopt his father's attitude and would deliver it to the Adirondacks.

YOUNG NAT

Nat and his brother, Lish, had to hunt in the woods for wild game to help feed their family while their father was away fighting the British. At nine years old, Nat obtained his first gun when he brokered a deal to bring in pelts to pay for it. He used this gun to take down large game, and though the recoil when he discharged his weapon would knock him flat onto his back, his marksmanship was remarkable. He brought down animals that he used to feed his family with jerk meat through the long winter. Lish was also a very good shot and trapper.

One time, a band of Indians came to their cabin and demanded water and jerked beef, so Nat's mother asked him to fetch the water while she gave them what she had in the main cabin, not telling them she had a hidden barrel in a shed in the back. Nat ran to a still-water scummy frog pond, filled the jug with rank water and brought it back. The lead Indian took a big swig of the water and bent over, vomiting it all over the ground. Unhappy at the trickery, the Indians tied young Nat to a tree while the leader held a tomahawk to his forehead and threatened to scalp the young lad. Nat's mother threw herself at the feet of the Indians and begged them to spare her son. She had promised all the jerked meat they had, and she took them over to the hidden barrel. The Indians took everything and left, and young Nat furiously swore he'd never let another Indian touch him.

Nat and Lish shot and killed all manner of animals like bear, wolves, deer and moose, but they had a memorable encounter with a bald eagle. They came upon a net they had used to try to trap a wolf and found an eagle stuck in the net. Nat built a cage to house the eagle, as it had a broken leg. Nat's clothes were shredded as he freed the eagle from the net and placed him in the cage. They named the eagle Old Put after General Putnam and eventually freed the eagle once his leg was healed.

Nat became friends with Mary Wilson, whose father, William Wilson, was the area Loyalist and was very wealthy. Mary had been shocked to discover that Nat could not read or write, which was not unusual in that time. Those who lived in the frontier didn't have time to learn to read and write; they had to survive and provide for their families. Mary and Nat were in a field picking blackberries when a mother bear and her cubs approached. The mother bear charged, and young Nat told Mary to run for it. He had only one load in his gun. He was calm as he carefully aimed his gun and discharged it as the bear was on top of him. The bear slumped over dead, and Nat ran to catch up with the frightened girl. He walked her back to her home, where William Wilson was so grateful that he offered to pay for Nat's education in Boston. The only catch was the lad had to swear loyalty to the Crown and renounce the Revolutionists. Nat's answer was, "My father is a rebel, and so am I." He stormed off the property and never wanted to see Mary or her Loyalist father again.

THE MOVE TO THE MOHAWK VALLEY

In 1782, the Revolutionary War was over and Nathanial Foster returned to his family after seven years and ten months of fighting. The war had ravaged his body, and his wife barely recognized the grizzled veteran, but as soon as she knew who it was, she threw her arms around her husband. The children flocked to their father, who was amazed to see how big and strong Nat, now sixteen, and Lish, eighteen, had become.

"Did you whip the Crown?" asked Nat. His father patted Nat on the back and replied, "Yes, my son." When told how Nat had been tied to a tree by the Indians, Nat's father took the time to instruct his boys on hating and shooting Indians.

Nathanial had fallen in love with the Mohawk Valley in New York State when he was fighting in the Battle of Oriskany and bragged about the beautiful landscape and plentiful game, along with the marvel of the Adirondack Mountains. The family discussed the decline of game in their present area, leading Nat and Lish to take longer excursions to find food, so Nathanial decided to move the entire family to the Mohawk Valley. Along the way, Nat asked his father if the Mohawk Valley and the Adirondacks had Injins. "There's plenty of them, son," replied the father. "I'll tell you, lad, that you make shooting them your life's work. Never excite or quarrel with any of them. Be kind and peaceful as you can as our maker made us. But it's different with Injins."

The Fosters sold all of their goods to make a light carry for relocation. On the move as the family got close to the Mohawk Valley, Nathanial noticed a few Indians following them. That night, he warned his sons to stay up and keep watch as the family slept next to the campfire. Nat sat hugging his gun in the shadows away from the campfire while everyone slept. He heard a twig snap, so he stood up. When he saw bushes move, he fired his gun into the shrubs, making the entire family jump awake. The next morning, they found blood where he had shot. It could've been wild game, but his father encouraged and embraced his son for shooting his first Indian, saying, "I reckon, Nat, that you made the daylight shine through one or two of the red devils."

The family settled in Johnstown, New York, right at the foothills of the Adirondacks. They built a log home on their chosen spot and quickly became friends with local settlers. Nat found the hunting exciting, as the area was teeming with wild game.

Another interaction with Indians would prove to be the turning point for Nat, making him hate them with the same intensity as his father. The entire family had gone to the nearest settlement for trade and commensuration, leaving Nat home with just his little sister, Zilpha, who was working outside. Nat was inside when a pack of ten Indians came out of the woods and grabbed Zilpha. Nat knew he only had the single bore with one shot in it, and he could never fight off the entire group, so he quickly hid in a crawl space under the floor and stayed silent as the Indians stole everything they could. He came out once he smelled smoke and discovered they had taken his little sister and set the Foster home on fire. Nat ran the two miles to the nearest settlement, where a posse was quickly put together. When getting back to their home, Nat was very upset that it was burned to the ground and declared, "I'll hate the red devils worse'n dad, and I'll shoot 'em every chance I get."

Apart from Nat and Lish, this was a group of adult men, but even Nathanial knew Nat was the best tracker of them all. That's saying something since all the men tracked and hunted game, but these were Indians who could disappear in a forest with no trace. Nat had seen the direction they had gone and quickly found their trail. Nat followed the Indians all day over rocks and through streams and woods and could tell they were walking single file and attempting to hide their tracks, but they could not lose Nat and the group. After tracking all day, Nat came to a halt. He climbed a large tree,

"This strange young man clad in buckskin"

Nat Foster in his Leatherstocking hunting outfit. *A.L. Byron-Curtiss.*

and he could see a small line of smoke. They knew that the Indians were either going to cook and eat a quick meal and then move on or camp there for the night. They'd have to sneak close enough to see. Nat crawled through the brush quietly and saw them eating a quick meal, and he saw Zilpha tied to a tree. The men had to attack now, so Nathanial explained tactics he had learned in the war, and the men came in from two sides and shot five of the Indians dead while the rest fled. Zilpha had been saved.

Nat, the Trapper and Hunter

At twenty-one, Nat had grown into a strong and powerful man, and he would disappear into the Adirondacks for months at a time to escape a life of farming. He felt that toiling the soil was for trapped men not free to roam, explore, trap, hunt and live off the rugged land. Nat's only companion on these excursions was his loyal dog, Rose, who reveled in following Nat on his woodland journeys. Lish had taken up with a woman and still occasionally joined his little brother, but most of the time it was just Nat.

On one excursion into the Adirondacks, Nat had set up a log camp on the shores of Piseco Lake and went out hunting from that base camp. He was out one day near Sacandaga River when Rose started to growl with all her fur standing on end. Nat calmed her down and hid in the brush. He watched a group of Indians walk by, so he kept Rose calm and watched so as to not stir anything up. They could have been peaceful Indians, but that illusion was shattered when he saw a little white girl in a torn dress being walked with the group. Nat was thirty miles from the nearest settlement and knew he'd have to try to save the child or die trying.

Nat went a mile down the path, leaving Rose with his pack. He came back in the dark and saw the Indians in their bedrolls when he stepped on a stick. The snap alerted the Indians, who came awake whooping. Luckily, a panther was in the tree above the Indians, and it growled and took off. The Indians pursued, so Nat rushed in, cut the girl free from her bonds and took off, saving her with no conflict. But that was not the end, for the Indians pursued Nat as he emptied his basket, put the girl in it and took off with his gun in his hands and her on his back. After a day of running, the Indians discovered him on a small hill. Nat fired his gun at the lead Indian, and they retreated as they heard other gunshots from the distance. Nat asked the girl's name, and she said it was Mary French and that she had been picking berries with her friends when she was snatched. The other gunfire had come from members of the search party who were overjoyed to see Nat. Mary's father rushed forward with tears in his eyes at the return of his dear little Mary.

It was later that year that Nat met and became a dear friend of the legendary tracker, hunter and woodsman Nicholas Stoner. Stoner brought Nat to St. Johnsville for an Independence Day celebration, where Nat won the footrace and defeated the country's best wrestler in a match. The locals were impressed by the young man in the buckskins and moccasins. After the feats of strength, people cried out that a man and his daughter had fallen into the river from their boat. Nat at once ran for the water and saved the lass from drowning. It turned out to be Mary Wilson and her Loyalist father. Nat would rebuff a reward offer, as he never forgot how Wilson had treated him as a youngster.

Three years later, Nat married Jemima Streeter, who was from St. Lawrence County where her father was a justice of the county. They settled in Salisbury, New York. His farm was 150 acres, and Nat grew many crops, yet the hunter and trapper in him still called him to the woods to get valuable furs and pelts. His farm was so bountiful that Nat was known in the winter to go on sleigh to poor neighbors and give them sacks of grain. He had a trout pond on the property and always brought out fresh fish for dinner. He stayed on the farm in Salisbury for thirty years and raised a large family. He would still go out on hunting excursions with Lish and his younger brothers, bagging panthers, wolves and black bears, along with trapping beaver, muskrats and otters. He would have traps all the way across the Adirondacks, from the southern tip through to St. Lawrence County.

One thing Nat was amazing at was firing his gun. He could discharge it six times in a minute, an incredible feat that he accomplished by keeping three well-paired balls between the fingers on each hand. He would pour the powder from his horn, roll the ball down the barrel without a patch, strike the butt of the gun with his hand and then fire. This only worked at short range, as having to patch and driving them home with a ramrod was necessary for longer shots. One time, a military detachment was passing through Salisbury and claimed to have the fastest, most accurate gunman in the military. After being challenged, Nat easily defeated this marksman, to the astonishment of the commanding officer. Nat was offered generous pay for enlistment but declined.

Nat was deep in the Adirondacks toward Fulton Chain when he was approached and shot at by a singular Indian. Nat took refuge behind a tree, and he and the Indian took turns shooting back and forth at each other throughout the afternoon without either getting an advantage. At dusk, Nat took off his coonskin hat and his coat, arranging them on a branch and holding them out from the tree until the Indian shot them through. Nat groaned as if he had been mortally wounded. The Indian took out his knife and bounded toward Nat, whooping with glee at his soon-to-be scalped trophy, when Nat stepped from behind the tree and shot the Indian through the forehead, dropping him dead in his tracks.

Nat's reputation as an Indian killer grew, but he was reluctant to talk about his exploits, let alone brag. He was a man who only killed them when he had no other choice, but Indians grew to resent his reputation and referred to him as Ole Nat Foster Indian Killer. Some sought him out. One Indian made the fatal mistake of walking up to Nat, who was with a few companions, and asking if they knew where Ole Nat Foster was. Nat gave a wink to his friends and asked what he wanted with Nat, and the Indian declared he was going to shoot him dead. Nat pointed to a nearby pond and stated that Nat's traps started over there. By the time the Indian realized his mistake, it was too late and he was dropped by a ball in the chest.

Nat had many interactions with Indians, but one of his most famous was with Indian Hess, who had fought for the Loyalists in the war and whom many considered the most bloodthirsty man in the country. Nat was in a tavern in Little Falls when he ran into Indian Hess. Nat would not reveal his name as the two men sat and drank at the bar together; eventually, they decided to go on a hunting excursion together. Despite Nat's killing of Indians, he never did so unless he had to and was friendly with all people, so it was not unusual for this to occur. Nat did not know the true nature of Indian Hess until they were in the woods together and Indian Hess was bragging about his exploits in the Revolutionary War, showing Nat a leather pouch that he claimed was made from the skin of an unborn child he had ripped out of the stomach of a pregnant woman. It wasn't until their parting that Indian Hess inquired about Nat's identity and, on hearing it, declared, "Ha! Nat Foster, you bad man, you kill Indians." Nat got the feeling that the Indian would kill him if given the opportunity, although they parted as not friends but not enemies either.

A short time later, Nat was out hunting and brought down a bull moose. As he got close to his prey, Indian Hess bounded from behind a tree with a tomahawk in his hand, whooping and closing in on Nat. Little did Indian Hess realize that Nat was the fastest loader in the world. He recharged his weapon in time to fire a shot on Indian Hess as soon as he was on top of him, thus ending the life of the old Indian war veteran.

Nat never once reveled in these matters, and his children and grandchildren would say he didn't like to talk about it, never saying he killed any Indians, only stating that he sent them back to Canada. He was a man who only shot Indians out of necessity as the time dictated. He was known to be friendly with many Indians but continued to have skirmishes. Nat had come to make many trips to the Fulton Chain of Lakes in Old Forge and had a camp on Eighth Lake, where he trapped up and down the entire chain. He noticed that his traps were being poached, so he hid with his canoe on First Lake and witnessed Indians taking his trappings and hiding them under some lakeside brush. He waited for them to leave and reclaimed his

"Another creature that often made things lively for our hero."

Indian Drid, whom Nat Foster was accused of killing. *A.L. Byron-Curtiss.*

items. Nat knew that once discovered, they might come for him, so he went about making a campsite and made a fake man out of twigs and covered the dummy with his hat and bedding. He sat back, hidden in the woods with his dog, Watch, and waited. In the night, he observed two Indians in a canoe as they paddled quietly to shore, got out, snuck up on the camp and fired their guns into the dummy. Nat didn't kill the Indians but shot in their direction. He scared them off and never saw them again.

THE END

Nat Foster fell in love with the Fulton Chain of Lakes and the Old Forge area, so he decided to rent his farm in Salisbury to his son Amos and moved to the area at sixty-five years old. In his new frontier homestead was an Indian by the name of Drid. He had heard of Nat's reputation as a killer of his race, so he went out of his way to pick a fight with the old woodsman. Drid once took Nat's boat down to the lake and sunk it. Nat found out and held Drid at gunpoint and made him take him to the location of the boat. When Nat was bent over inspecting it, Drid pulled his knife. Nat, although much older, was able to fight off the Indian and gain his weapon. Nat refused to shoot Drid and told him to be gone. Although he had a quarrel with Drid, Nat and his wife were generous to Drid's squaw and children, providing them with milk free of charge and other foodstuffs.

Nat was no longer interested in shooting Indians and tried his best to avoid conflict, although Drid had threatened to shoot and kill Nat on several occasions. New laws had been passed to protect Indians from slaughter, so Nat went to local justice of the peace Joshua Harris, who would not swear out a warrant for Drid as the man was well known and feared by many. He suggested Nat move from the area to get away from the menacing Indian. "What!" said Nat. "After I've hunted the red devils for over thirty years, be scared away by one? If you won't give me protection, then I'll do it myself." The argument between Nat and Drid reached a climax when the two got into a scuffle that ended with Drid pulling a knife and cutting Nat's arm before two men broke up the fight.

Nat decided he'd have to shoot the Indian and ended up doing it on a popular spot in the Fulton Chain where there were possible witnesses, unlike his other shootings where he was alone with his victims in the woods. Nat was standing in brush along the lake while Drid was in his canoe. One load report, and the Indian slumped over dead. This time, Nat would be charged in the crime. This was the only indictment Nat Foster had in his life for killing an Indian. Judge Segar from Turin listened to the facts of the case and swore out a warrant. Nat was placed under arrest and held in the jail in the village of Martinsburg. Since the crime took place in Herkimer County, Nat was transferred to the Herkimer County Jail in Herkimer, New York. He was charged with murder on February 3, 1834. During the trial, there was no actual witness who could testify that Nat shot Drid. Witnesses had seen him on the point and shore area right before the shot and heard it, yet none had seen him pull the trigger. Drid had many enemies. The jury found Nat

Foster not guilty of murder. Applause erupted in the courtroom, and Nat stood up, smiled with his hands over his head and said, "God bless you all." The crowd rushed him, picked him up over their heads and marched him through the streets of Herkimer.

Nat eventually left his beloved Old Forge and Mohawk Valley, retreating to Wilkes-Barre, Pennsylvania, to live amongst relatives. He was hunting in that state when he had a heart attack. He lived but was greatly weakened, so he returned to Ava, New York, to spend his last days with his daughter Jemima. He lasted one more year before passing away in his sleep on March 16, 1840, when he was buried in the Quaker Cemetery in Ava. A.L. Byron-Curtiss suggested in his book *The Life and Adventures of Nat Foster, Trapper and Hunter of the Adirondacks* that James Fenimore Cooper had based the character Natty Bumppo from his Leatherstocking Tales, including the famous *Last of the Mohicans*, on Nat Foster. Nat's descendants certainly felt this way, since many of Nat's legendary tales seemed to be similar to those featured in Cooper's books, including the fact Nat was called "Leatherstocking" by many in Salisbury. One thing is for sure: Nat Foster lived a life still recalled by his descendants and admirers, who have ensured that his amazing adventures have stood the test of time.

Chapter 2
Slaves in the Mountains

"Americas First Domestic Terrorist."
—*Ken Chowder's description of John Brown as written in* American Heritage

HARPERS FERRY

John Brown is considered one of the leading abolitionists before the outbreak of the Civil War. He is especially well known for the raid he led on a United States arsenal at Harpers Ferry in Virginia in 1859, an event that many felt led to a deeper division between the North and the South and ultimately the outbreak of the Civil War and the eventual freedom of slaves. Many in the South refer to John Brown as the first domestic terrorist in the United States, while many in the North refer to him as a hero and a martyr. There is no doubt that feelings run deep on both sides even to this day, but the fact of the matter is that John Brown was steadfast against his fellow man being chained in bondage as slaves. His raid on Harpers Ferry was his and his team's attempt to take over the armory that housed over 100,000 rifles and muskets. He wanted to arm the slaves, allowing them to revolt against their masters. A handful of Brown's men, including two of his sons, were killed in the raid. John Brown was hanged for his crime, and his body was brought to North Elba, New York, and buried in a grave not far from Lake Placid, in the midst of the Adirondack Mountains. It was the utopian escaped slave settlement that John Brown tried to establish that eventually led him to the Adirondack Mountains.

Famous depiction of John Brown titled *Tragic Prelude*, by John Steuart Curry. On display in the Kansas state capitol. *Courtesy legendsofamerica.com.*

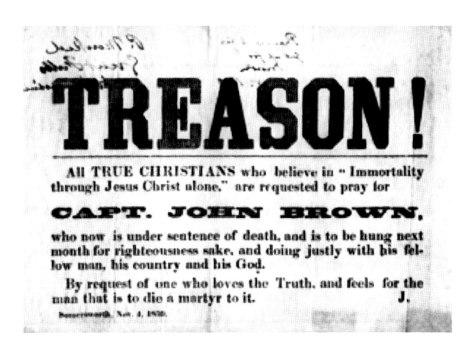

A poster asking the public to pray for the condemned abolitionist John Brown, who had been sentenced to hang. *Theamericanscholar.org.*

A Meeting with Gerrit Smith

The year was 1848, and John Brown had heard of the abolitionist Gerrit Smith and the land he was giving to escaped slaves in the Adirondacks. John Brown traveled to Peterboro, New York, to meet the champion of freedom. Brown sat down with Smith and explained to him that he wanted to relocate his family to the Adirondacks, establish a farm and create a community where he could assist and guide the escaped slaves in a new life in the rugged mountains. Smith wholeheartedly accepted the proposal from John Brown and agreed to sell him property for one dollar per acre.

The Slave Settlement

John Brown, his family and other abolitionists brought escaped southern slaves through the Underground Railroad up to the rugged land in North Elba. They took in families of slaves, building them cottages and giving each family an acre of their own land. John and his sons attempted to teach the escaped slaves how to build an industry, how to survive in the unfamiliar terrain and how to be self-sufficient.

John Brown's Homestead, painting by Robert D. Wilkie, showing John Brown's estate in the Adirondacks.

The utopian society named "Negro Republic" that John Brown had envisioned was doomed from the start. The very first winter was extremely harsh, and the slaves coming from the South were used to hot and humid conditions—not the nasty, cold, bitter winds and extreme conditions in the Adirondack Mountain range. The escaped slave families had extreme famine that first winter as provisions stocked in cellars were used up and the amount of prepared firewood to warm the cottages from the brutal Adirondack Mountain winter winds was not enough to stave off the many months of deep freeze and sub-zero temperatures. On top of the food shortages and severe cold, the escaped slaves had an outbreak of measles and scarlet fever that caused many of them to lose their lives. John Brown and his sons would spend the entire winter bringing in sleds of provisions through monstrous snowdrifts to the escaped slave families. This allowed many of them to survive that first winter, but when the spring thaw came, the slave families broke away from their utopian community and dispersed throughout Adirondack villages and Canadian towns, thus leaving John Brown and his sons to oversee what remained of the settlement.

The Meeting of Legends

John Brown remained a resident of North Elba for many years and often left to meet with legendary abolitionists Gerrit Smith and Frederick Douglass. It

John Brown hanging. John Wilkes Booth was among the witnesses. This drawing is held at the Virginia Military Institute archives. *Courtesy Adirondack Almanack, adirondackalmanack.com.*

was at one of these meetings that John Brown declared that he and his sons would be "warriors of the Lord against the mighty wicked" and that he was seeking "free soldiers" of color who would fight against the "border ruffians" of Missouri and Kansas. John Brown's death would serve as a rallying cry for many Union soldiers and became a chant and song titled "John Brown's Body" that they would sing in their marches about "John Brown's body mouldering in a grave."

LASTING LEGACY

Abolitionist John Brown.

John Brown had committed illegal acts by harboring and assisting escaped slaves and attempting to make their own settlement in the Adirondack Mountains. Many in the South would refer to him as a murderer or a terrorist; however, there is no doubting the man believed in equality of all humans, regardless of the color of their skin, and he believed that the use of fellow human beings in bondage for slavery was a sin in the eyes of God. The man paid the ultimate sacrifice and died for his beliefs. John Brown's North Elba residence would be owned by New York State in 1895 and preserved as a state park. John Brown's body was returned to the Adirondacks and buried in North Elba, near Lake Placid, along with twelve men who had died at Harpers Ferry. The names are engraved on a large boulder on the site, which also contains a statue of John Brown walking with his arms around a young African American lad. This spot is one of the most visited in the

Adirondack Park. John Brown broke many laws and polarized many Americans, but he was a champion of human rights and deserves his place amongst legends of our country who sacrificed everything so that others may enjoy freedom.

Chapter 3
Mad Father Craven

"The terrible trouble existing between the Catholic Church and their former pastor, John Craven, had a terrible ending on the 8th day of September, a day not soon to be forgotten, and the murder committed not to be effaced from the remembrance of witnesses."
—*an announcement made upon the murder charge given to Father John Craven, Constableville, 1876*

There exists no greater trust and admiration in any community than that granted to a man of the cloth. Catholic priests dedicate their lives to the service of God and the members of the parish community of which they are assigned. When one falls from God and the moral course, the outcomes are tragic, and in the case of Father John Craven, this path would prove to be downright crazy and deadly.

In the late nineteenth century, the hamlets of Constableville and Highmarket had a new priest assigned to St. Mary's, the little Catholic church nestled in a place of convenience for all in both communities to worship the Lord. It was this place that the bishop of the district assigned Father John Craven to be the new priest, a man who had been ordained at the seminary in Troy, New York. Father Craven brought his mother and his brother, Patrick, to stay with him, having previously been the pastor at Olmsteadville, Redwood and Clayton, all places where he had led parishioners with all the grace and spiritual drama his office allowed. He would save all his high drama and insane theatrics for the common and decent folks of the Constableville and Highmarket areas.

Mad Father Craven

It was not be known until later that Father Craven's brother had previously been institutionalized in insane asylums in Buffalo and Poughkeepsie. This affliction was in the family strain, and it was brought out of Father Craven after a near fatal accident.

Father Craven's service to Constableville had begun with nary a dramatic event or oddity. Unfortunately, he was thrown from a horse-and-buggy and clunked his head upon solid sod that rattled his brain and brought out a different man, a pastor who would begin to act unconventionally and whose antisocial antics would stun and terrorize the parishioners. Father Craven's mental deterioration wasn't helped by a lone resident of the area who played a cruel trick on the priest by "docking" his horse's tail, along with other unnamed mental and physical cruelties that did nothing but inflame a deep-seated mental disability.

Father Craven then married, a move that is against the Catholic Church doctrine. He was suspended by the bishop, but he continued to stand at the lectern, railing against the church and the bishop by declaring, "I am St. Mary's Church!" Wiping the sweat beads away from his forehead and gripping the podium with white knuckles, he spewed out at his stunned parishioners, "I possess sole ecclesiastical power! I have excommunicated the Pope!" As Father Craven's insane rants ratcheted upward, his Mass attendance spiraled downward.

Eventually, these events would escalate to murder. It all began with a tiny spark from a nearby brush fire in a field that touched the wooden walls of St. Mary's on May 14, 1879. This fire spread and burned the little church in the pretty little village right down to the root of the stone foundation, as if God himself had reached down and took care of what mortal men would not, getting Father Craven away from his bully pulpit. Although the bishop had suspended Father Craven just four days before the fire, the fearful citizens and local authorities did nothing to force him away from the church before or after the fire that left nothing but the stone foundation. He continued to live near the burned foundation with his mother and brother and fiercely guarded the place, chasing away any who dared come near. Father Craven even left evidence of his mental decline on paper when he wrote a defiant letter to the Catholic Church treasurer of New York State demanding $75,000 for the rebuilding of St. Mary's Church. Dr. Douglas of Constableville came forward and offered his medical opinion on the mental decline of Father Craven by stating, "I noticed a change in Father Craven's appearance after his marriage, from being a gentleman to something that begat slovenly and violent behavior. Father Craven is unsafe to be in our midst."

The tragic rule and unpredictable run of Father John Craven came to an end in September 1881. A parishioner had gone to the burnt-out church and attempted to remove a foundation stone, a move that sent Father Craven into a rage. The excommunicated priest attacked the man, who fled and filed assault charges. Constable Issacs came out to the site of the assault and attempted to serve Father Craven with a warrant, but he was verbally assaulted and intimidated by Father Craven and his brother, Patrick. Constable Issacs wisely retreated back to the village in order to gather additional resources, for he alone was no match for the two Craven brothers. He returned with Nelson Felshaw, R.E. Conant and Addison Clover. When the posse of four men arrived, Father Craven and his brother had dug a trench inside the foundation of the church and both stood at the ready armed with large, sharp, menacing scythes. The constable and his men had a standoff as the lawman tried to reason with the armed men. Father Craven yelled out, "I will harm anyone crossing the ditch! The warrant is defective!"

Barney Egan, a resident of nearby Highmarket, witnessed this standoff and tense exchange. He asked Constable Issacs, "Why don't you arrest these men? If you are afraid then I will do it alone." Egan walked to the cemetery that was adjacent to the burnt-out St. Mary's Church, returned with a small picket and took steps toward the Cravens. Patrick Craven took this as a sign of assault and jumped over the trench, out of the burnt-out foundation and toward Egan. Faced with an insane man with an oversized implement, Egan dropped his picket and attempted to flee, but it was too late. Patrick hacked the man down with a powerful blow. The killer repeated the blows over and over until Barney Egan lie hacked to pieces in a puddle of blood that soiled the holy ground. Patrick retreated and, with his brother, continued to verbally menace the constable and his men who were now busy picking up the pieces of the dead man and placing him in a wagon. They took his remains to Dr. Douglas's office, where he declared the obvious: Egan was dead, and his soul had departed this world.

Constable Issacs returned with greater numbers and took the Cravens into custody. He placed them both under arrest and took them to the county jail in Lowville, New York, where both were charged with murder. An announcement was made by law officials after the arrest of Father Craven: "The terrible trouble existing between the Catholic Church and their former pastor, John Craven, had a terrible ending on the 8th day of September, a day not soon to be forgotten, and the murder committed not to be effaced from the remembrance of witnesses." In the criminal trial, Patrick Craven would be found guilty by the jury and Father John Craven would be found guilty of aiding and abetting his brother in the deadly deed. It was after the trial that three men would decide the fate of the brothers. Dr. John P. Gray, Honorable Henry R. Turner and Dr. William Johnson met the two convicted murderers and, after interview and discussion amongst themselves, declared the Craven brothers insane. Both were committed to the insane asylum in Utica. St. Mary's was rebuilt on the same spot but succumbed to not one but two more fires in 1885 and 1887, as if Father Craven had placed a curse on the spot. Father Craven was eventually transferred to a Catholic hospital for the insane in Canada, where he spent the rest of his life, miles away from his beloved pulpit.

Chapter 4
Don't Steal the Timber

"Eternal vigilance is the pride of public forests."
—*special correspondence to the* New York Evening Post, *October 30, 1905*

THE NEW YORK STATE
FOREST COMMISSION EDITORIAL

Conservation and preservation of the Adirondack Mountain forests is nothing new. Residents and lovers of the trees have been passionate about their protection as far back as the late nineteenth century, when public outcry occurred as three members of the New York State Forest Commission granted New York Central Railroad rights to clear-cut thousands of acres through virgin Adirondack forests in order to make a train path from Malone to Herkimer. An editorial in the Thursday, May 14, 1891 edition of the *New York Herald* blasted the Forest Commission and called for the commissioners' removal by Governor David B. Hill. The three commissioners were called unfit and immoral for their allowance of a swath to be cut in the Adirondack forest by New York Central Railroad, and the overseer of the project, Dr. W. Seward Webb, was chastised for his lobbying the commission and being granted permission to chop trees. This path would strike into the mainline of the railroad and provide important commerce to the northern territory, but to champions of the grand Adirondacks, it was tantamount to an act of treason against the beauty of the forest.

Don't Steal the Timber

The editorial started out by stating that "the Adirondack forest will soon disappear. Goodbye to the Adirondacks for the fate of the noble forest is sealed. A beautiful forest is a dream of the past." The fact that these words were printed in a pro–forest preservation editorial in 1891 shows the passion people had for the beauty of the trees and landscape. The *New York Herald* called the three members of the forest commission "a miserable trio of evil men that put the forest in peril." The *Herald* stated that the New York Central Railroad had already clear-cut thousands of trees using two thousand Italian immigrant laborers. The clear-cutting had been going on, and the public outcry didn't deter the Forest Commission, which yielded great power in its position. The Webb Road was eventually built, and the *Herald* publicly and in print called the commission members "cowards" and a "rotten commission," although the railroad eventually secured the right of way regardless. The *Herald* was afraid that the commission would turn over the entire "people's woods" to the railroad. This would cause a complete clear-cut, leaving a scarred and blighted landscape. The *Herald* asked Governor Hill to reorganize the Forest Commission and remove the three commissioners, for the *Herald* argued that the commissioners neglected their duty and were unjustly enriched by money from the sales of the cut timber and by turning the right of way over to the railroads.

Despite the heavy-handed editorial, the *New York Herald* was unsuccessful at stopping the progress of the railroad; however, in addition to this

Some Adirondack guides were viewed as squatters on New York State property. *www.Adirondack-history.com.*

editorial, businessmen in the community also came forward and demanded a regulated tree-cutting program since clearing out all the trees could lead to erosion of silt that would clog important rivers like the Hudson, thus hindering river commerce. The New York State Legislature established the Adirondack Park in 1892 to protect the pristine forest. This would give the trees state constitutional protection and keep the park forever wild. Unfortunately, this would not end the illegal theft of timber. Today, over one million acres of the forest is deemed wilderness, yet it continues to be challenged, and trees are poached to this day.

TRESPASSERS AND SQUATTERS

The year was 1905, and New York State Governor Frank W. Higgins made a public statement that the taking of any logs from the Adirondack state land was a violation of state law and state constitution and those parties that perpetrated such a deed would be charged and the illegally taken timber seized. A big issue arose when state log detectives investigated and moved to seize what they thought was illegally taken timber, but the logs were not branded and thus not able to be proven taken from the Adirondack forest. In an article from April 1905, the *New York Herald* claimed New York State authorities were negligent in their duty to protect the trees and timber. On top of that, it was discovered that trespassers were going onto state land and taking away dead trees sitting on the ground, and squatters and guides were living illegally on protected Adirondack territory. The *Herald* called on the state to go after the timber thieves, trespassers and squatters along with the officials who allowed it and to protect the forest under the law.

The heavy pressure from investigative journalists caused the New York Assembly to conduct an investigation in which committee members drove throughout the Adirondack Mountains discovering people taking fallen timber off state-protected property, as well as dozens of camps, summer homes and permanent residential houses illegally planted on protected forest. This included boating out to islands that hosted illegal shacks. The assembly committee had discovered that the illegal structures were either owned by locals or that the town had profited by supplying all manner of goods and services to the squatters and trespassers. These people had assumed it was perfectly fine to live on state land and take fallen trees since they were already dead and on the ground, but they were wrong. This discovery and exposé by the committee and pointed out by the *Herald* put a renewed emphasis on the protection of the Adirondack virgin forest that was under the protection of state law. Unfortunately, the pillage and violation would continue.

Power Companies

In 1905, the *Evening Post* printed an editorial chastising power companies that had applied to place dams on Saranac, Racquette and Sacondaga Rivers in order to generate hydroelectric power to surrounding communities while at the same time endangering tracts of timber. The editorial stated that "eternal vigilance is the pride of public forests." The *Post* claimed that many wardens of the Adirondacks had taken money from many of the over five hundred timber mills, paper mills, pulp mills and acid mills to look the other way while timber was plundered and trees exploited. That had been a blight on the law to protect the Adirondack forest, and now power companies were moving in. The *Post* stated that the power companies looked at the Adirondacks "with the emotion of a soldier on a visit to London who when he first looked on that rich city said, 'What a city to sack!'" The *Post* claimed that millions of feet of timber had been taken illegally, and the allowance of the power companies to construct these dams was another slap in the face of the Adirondack preservation law. There would be people who resided in the townships of the proposed dams who would lobby that generated electricity was needed to grow the area and provide an enhanced quality of life for residents and businesses. The power companies had stated that the only trees that would be eliminated would be the bed of the reservoirs. Debates like these still continue to this day and spark heightened emotions on the sides of those committed to the protection of the Adirondack Park and those who seek progress and lifestyle enhancement.

The Whipple Resignation

The continued debate and charges of illegal taking of timber reached an emotional peak in the fall of 1910 with the resignation of James Whipple, head of the New York State Forest, Fish and Game Commission. This resignation came after the investigation committee conducted an inquiry and determined that Whipple did not perform the full duty of his office. Whipple claimed in a letter to the governor that neither he nor his department did anything wrong, other than leave decisions in the hands of subordinates who made mistakes. As the head of the department for six years, he took full responsibility and resigned. The governor wrote back to Whipple in a letter made available to the public, where the governor thanked the commissioner for his service and confirmed that he hadn't purposefully done anything illegal; however, the conditions that had existed under his guidance needed to be addressed and rectified.

What were the findings of the investigation? Commissioners Roger Clark and H. Leroy Austin sent to the governor a report of their investigation in which they had interviewed hundreds of people and scoured thousands of records involving land purchases in the Adirondacks, along with the collection of funds for permits, hunting licenses, fees, fines and other miscellaneous collections. This money was not properly placed in an

Beavers had been considered costly to the precious Adirondack timber.

accurate accounting system, and there was shoddy record keeping. Laxness and lackadaisical record keeping was rampant throughout the Forest, Fish and Game Commission. Also, charges of political favoritism came out when forest fires were determined to have been caused by the railroads. Whipple's employees failed their fiduciary duty when they originally failed to charge or fine the railroads. After exposure, they imposed marginal fines, and the sums collected were much less than the state was entitled to. One of Whipple's assigned employees was in compliance in the department while also being employed by a paper mill that had been granted timber consideration. This was a blatant conflict of interest, and this employee voluntarily resigned his position. Another maneuver cited by the committee was the foot-dragging or outright refusal to prosecute from certain commissioners who knew of hundreds of squatters living on Adirondack state lands illegally. In Whipple's term in office, only a handful had judgments brought against them for eviction, with no one actually removed. These squatters included farmers, woodsmen, guides and very wealthy men of industry who had erected permanent homes on state lands. The last and most devastating straw was that Commissioner Whipple's appointed employees, whose job it was to safeguard the trees, had allowed clear-cutting to continue even after squatters had a judgment against them to vacate the area they were taking timber from. There was lazy follow-up with correspondence instead of site visits and shoddy record keeping. Neither Commissioner Whipple nor any of his state employees was charged, but the searing publicized report led to dozens of resignations, including Whipple's, and a call by the governor to revamp and improve the record keeping, running and supervision of the entire Forest, Fish and Game Commission.

Blame It on the Beavers

A study was done by the Roosevelt Wild Life Forest Experiment Station of the New York College of Forestry–Syracuse University in 1925 that listed the destruction of Adirondack forest trees by beavers. The insidious swimming rodents had been gnawing trees and flooding out others, causing considerable damage. Dr. Charles Eugene Johnson, fur naturalist for the station, conducted a thorough investigation of the beaver problem in the Adirondacks. Dr. Johnson gave a detailed report on the number of trees cut down by beavers and the damage done by them and offered solutions to eradicate the tree-killing mammals. The dam building of the beavers caused damage to the forest as rivers and streams turned into flood plains. Dr. Johnson personally measured a tree of seventeen inches that had been cut down by the yellow incisors of the tail-slapping, pernicious beasts. He listed the trees Adirondack beaver found most tasty to be aspen, poplar and yellow birch. Dr. Johnson declared that the damage done by timber cutters was relatively small compared to the apocalyptic chewing of the beaver. He claimed most of the trees were destroyed when the beaver dams flooded an area and drowned and killed trees in the beaver dam flood plain. Dr. Johnson estimated that in 1923, beavers had caused tree damage in the Adirondacks to roughly $25,000 or roughly $3 per beaver dam.

His solution? Kill the beaver! Dr. Johnson estimated that there were roughly 8,000 beavers in the Adirondacks and that a hunting program could yield 3,500 pelts a year without any diminishment to the population. Between the revenue of the pelts and the savings of damaged trees, the beaver eradication program would yield annual capital of $500,000. So the next time you hear a chainsaw buzzing through a pristine Adirondack aspen, don't fret of the environmental damage; just think of the beaver and all the trees they're destroying with their large sharp yellow incisors.

The Adirondack Park Agency

Many decades after the scandal and resignation of Commissioner Whipple, trees continued to be illegally cut down and fallen timber taken illegally from the Adirondack Park. Even as recently as 1972, a development firm had clear-cut thousands of trees illegally and was investigated by the state. This, along with many other infractions, caused New York State to create the Adirondack Park Agency, which signed an agency master plan in 1973. The mission was to protect the private and public land in the Adirondacks through the law. The mission of the Adirondack Park Agency is administered by three statutes: 1) the Adirondack Park Agency Act 2) the New York State Freshwater Wetlands Act and 3) the New York State Wild, Scenic and Recreational Rivers System Act. No system is perfect, and there have certainly been disagreements over the years on proper land use, but all involved agree that preservation of the Adirondacks and protection of its trees, water and landscape are vital to the health of New York State and the nation.

Chapter 5
The Windfall Gang

"If I ever get the chance, I'm gonna get even with him."
—*Benjamin Wadsworth, talking about his younger brother, William Wadsworth*

The James Gang was the most famous family criminal enterprise in the history of the West, and the Loomis Gang ruled central New York with its cunning criminal brood, yet there once existed a family crime gang in the Adirondack Mountains in the late nineteenth and early twentieth centuries. However, they came across more like the gang who couldn't shoot straight rather than like their more successful crime family predecessors.

The Windfall Gang was a family enterprise made up of the Wadsworth clan. They were all large men, well over six feet tall and muscular, and this group included William, Charles, Daniel and Benjamin, as well as their criminal friend Edward McGuire. They were named after the town where they had been born.

The ringleader was Charles Wadsworth, and he led the robbery of Hosley's General Store in Wells, New York, in the fall of 1898. Charles waited with the rest of the Windfall Gang until dark, when he snuck up to the cellar window and busted it out. He slithered inside and unlocked the front door, allowing his criminal family and friend to loot and pillage the store. The Windfall Gang was suspected and on the run until Charles was captured in dramatic fashion.

He had eluded capture until June 1899, when Deputy Sheriff William Osborne, of Speculator, and a small posse were searching the area of Indian Lake, where they had a tip the fugitive had been hiding out. They got their break when they stood watch in cover of woods at the house of Charles's wife. Soon the fugitive arrived, the sheriff and his posse moved in and a scuffle ensued. Charles Wadsworth was large and powerful, so he easily overpowered the posse and took flight, but Sheriff Osborne shot Charles in the arm, disabling the criminal mastermind. The posse and the sheriff then easily subdued the man, wrapping his injury, getting him medical attention and then taking him by a two-horse wagon, where Sheriff Osborne sat with his double-barrel shotgun, to the Lake Pleasant jail. The rest of the Windfall Gang eluded capture for a while longer but eventually were caught and charged with the robbery. Edward McGuire turned state evidence and testified in Hamilton County Court against the rest of the Windfall Gang in exchange for a one-year sentence in Dannemora Prison from Judge McGann. The rest of the gang pleaded not guilty and were sent back to jail to await their trial.

It was during this stay in prison that the Adirondack desperados made a bold escape. Benjamin and William Wadsworth had been granted time in the prison yard to do some chores under the watchful eye of a guard. In the few seconds that the guard took his eyes off the brothers, they managed to flee into the woods. Sheriff Perkins formed a posse and gave chase to the two escaped fugitives, searching the area until dark. They added more members to the posse the following morning and resumed their search in Lake Pleasant and toward the town of Wells. The posse went to David Wadsworth's sawmill in Wells, where they hid in the pine woods and quietly waited. Suddenly, they saw one of their suspects running from the sawmill into the woods carrying a weapon. The posse spread out and surrounded the desperate and dangerous outlaw. The sheriff and his men recognized the fugitive as Benjamin Wadsworth, who refused to stop running but, once cornered by dozens of armed volunteers, threw his weapon to the ground and gave up. He was taken back to jail at Lake Pleasant and refused to talk about his younger brother, William. It was well known that Benjamin had told many people that he would get even with his brother for testifying against the family. William had talked at first and then changed his mind once the court dates were set, but the damage had already been done. Sheriff Perkins and other law officers felt that Benjamin had murdered his younger brother for betraying the family, but he refused to talk or give any information, including where he had acquired the gun he was carrying when captured. William's body has never been found, and Benjamin was not charged with murder, as there was no evidence such a crime took place. The Windfall Gang members who had yet to be sentenced would plead guilty to burglary in the third degree and were sentenced to prison. In the Supreme Court at Lake Pleasant, the Wadsworth men were brought into court heavily manacled about the wrists and ankles, for many feared the massive, strong criminals. The zenith of the court proceedings occurred when Assistant District Attorney Cunningham asked Charles Wadsworth, ringleader of both the family and Windfall Gang, his plea. Charles stood and said, "The most dreaded word in my vocabulary…guilty." The Windfall Gang would not go down in history as one of the well-known crime families, but for a sliver of time, they did create havoc and fear in the Adirondacks.

Chapter 6
The Great Adirondack Stagecoach Robbery

"No harm will come to you if you keep quiet and hand over whatever available cash you have."
—*armed stagecoach robber, speaking to the female passengers left behind*

When you think of stagecoach robberies, visions of the Wild West come to mind: bandits with masks and cactus and Indians in the background. You wouldn't think of tall pine trees and scenic Adirondack roadways, yet it happened. On one fateful day in August 1901, a stagecoach carrying wealthy passengers from New York City heading into the mountains for a relaxing summer vacation was met by a couple men with guns and no hesitation to pull the trigger. The stagecoach was pulled by a team of four horses and had sacks of mail, express packages and seven passengers, four men and three women. The driver of the stagecoach was William "Bill" Eldridge. The stagecoach was between North Creek and Blue Mountain Lake Village in one of the most remote and wildest parts of the Adirondacks. The passengers were enjoying the summer day as the horses pulled them along the set path when two masked men jumped from the woods and held out their rifles. Bill Eldridge tried to continue, but the robbers shot and killed the two lead horses, making the stagecoach stop so suddenly that the elderly driver was thrown off his seat and to the ground, where he groaned in injury. One of the robbers stuck his head into the stagecoach window and pointed his gun, letting the passengers know to come on out. One of the ladies shrieked in hysteria. The passengers slowly came out of the stagecoach, and one by one, the men handed over

Stagecoach robberies have always been a part of popular culture, including many movies and television shows.

their valuables and money, then they all bolted for the woods—except one husband, who changed his mind and came back to stand by his wife when she grabbed him by the coattails and halted his progress. The other three male passengers fled like cowards and left the remaining brave women to stand up and be stolen from. One robber stood back and held his gun on the victims. The robbers did not follow the men into the woods and told the ladies that no harm would come to them if they were quiet and handed over their possessions. Nobody said a word as they cooperated fully while one of the robbers went through the pockets of the driver, who was still groaning in pain on the ground. The group then stood back as one robber opened every single letter and pocketed whatever cash there was, along with anything else he deemed of value. He then opened all the express packages and took whatever was of value that he could carry in a single shoulder bag. The two stagecoach robbers walked slowly backward, keeping their guns on the victims as they slowly retreated into the woods and silently disappeared. The men would not come out of their hiding spot in the woods until the robbers and their wives were long gone.

Bill Eldridge picked himself up off the ground, cut loose the two dead horses and drove the passengers back to Dunlap's Hotel in North River, where the story of the robbery was revealed. Sometime later, the men who had fled into the woods returned to the hotel. The haul that the stagecoach robbers had acquired was valued around $1,000, yet the small safe that was under the coachman's seat had been overlooked. It was also revealed that Bill Eldridge had smartly hidden a roll of money that had belonged to the stagecoach company in his pants. The robbers never discovered the $400, instead only grabbing the $20 that Bill still had in his pocket. The passengers explained that they had boarded the stagecoach in Saratoga after coming from different areas. The names of the male passengers were Edward Bernstein and J.A. Laffey, of New York City; Edward Marquette, of Meriden, Connecticut; and John Case, of Blue Mountain Lake. Marquette was the lone man who stayed with his wife.

Upon hearing this tale, the locals mentioned that a stranger had stayed at Dunlap's Hotel. They remembered him as a large, stocky man who had left earlier that morning carrying a fishing rod, a small satchel and his rifle. The man had not given his name to the hotel, and they all felt he must have been one of the robbers. William Waddell, who operated the stagecoach line, called on the local citizens to form a posse and pursue the robbers. Many came forward, including highly skilled mountain men and trackers. The two robbers had a head start and must have been mountain men in their own right, for neither their trail nor the men was ever discovered. So be careful as you traverse the outlander areas of the Adirondack wilderness, for the ghosts of the stagecoach robbers just might hold you up and take all your worldly possessions.

Chapter 7
A Bad Man in the Adirondack Jungle

"With Pasco's death the last of the much feared Pasco Gang, which has terrorized the northern part of Warren County for fifty years, is gone."
—*reporter for the* Albany Evening Journal, *May 4, 1918*

Sam Pasco was a mountain man who was a mountain *of* a man, well over six feet in height and built like a black bear with a thick neck, legs and arms and massive hands that could snap a man's neck like a twig. In addition to being a rather large man, he was also an expert woodsman and deadeye with his gun. This was no gentle giant. The large mountaineer stood in court in Lake George under heavily armed guard, chained as only a wild vicious beast would be. The authorities had captured Pasco and charged him with the setting of over twenty forest fires, all within the blue line of the Adirondacks. When Pasco stood in court at Lake George, he was also charged with stealing timber, assault in the first degree and burglary in the third degree. The reporters at the time referred to Sam Pasco as "a bad man in the Adirondack jungle," and he certainly lived up to his reputation. Pasco pleaded not guilty to all the charges but was found guilty by his peers and sentenced to four years in Dannemora Prison by Judge Kiley. Pasco glared at the judge on his sentencing and declared he would kill him when he was freed.

The Pasco Gang consisted of a long line of criminals, but it all started with Sam's father, Leander Pasco, who was shot and killed by Calvin Wood in what the law had referred to back then as the "Warren County Feud." Calvin Wood received the death penalty for the murder, yet Sam never forgot it and vowed to take revenge on Calvin Wood's entire family. Sam Pasco's uncle, Charles Pasco, was shot and killed by Squire Barber when he was robbing the farmer's henhouse. Sam Pasco was released from Dannemora Prison after serving four years, and it took very little time before the big, bad man was in trouble again. In 1910, he had a quarrel with a neighbor, Ramann Walsey, over the placement of a fence. Sam Pasco was shot by a hidden person while walking his land. Walsey denied involvement and was never charged, as there were no witnesses.

Surgeons barely saved the life of Pasco, who learned nothing from the ordeal and went on to murder an innocent person. Sam had a disagreement with his brother-in-law in the spring of 1918 and shot Orley Eldridge in cold blood. The New York State police tracked down Sam Pasco and waited for the man to come out of the woods, figuring he would run out of food. Troopers Kelly and Herrick cornered Pasco, and the large mountain man opened fire, wounding Herrick, though not mortally. The troopers were joined by Trooper Grimly, and they again tracked Pasco, who took refuge in the cabin of E.T. Hewett, keeping the man as a hostage while the starved beast sat and ate all the provisions he could stuff into his bearded, bloated, murderous face. Pasco told Hewett that if he tried to escape or call out, he would kill him.

The troopers pulled back and hid in separate thickets surrounding the cabin and patiently waited for Sam Pasco. They knew the man would grow angry and impatient, and they were soon rewarded when Pasco came out of the cabin with his shotgun blazing round after round into the surrounding woods. It was midnight, and Pasco could not see the troopers, who returned fire, peppering the large man's body with multiple bullets. Sam Pasco walked off the porch of the cabin, lumbered two steps and slumped dead on the ground. The *Albany Evening Journal* reported on the gunfire exchange and Sam Pasco's death by declaring in print, "With Pasco's death the last of the much feared Pasco Gang, which has terrorized the northern part of Warren County for fifty years, is gone." The people of the county and the Adirondacks could sleep easier knowing the big, bad man was no longer of this mortal realm. The gunfire and fatal conclusion would not be forgotten, and the bravery of the New York State troopers was chronicled in a June 1945 edition of *Front Page Detective*, which featured the story of the hunt for "Bad Man" Sam Pasco.

Chapter 8

Millionaire Land Baron Assassination

"It was a well-planned crime and the work of an expert marksman."
—*George Winslow, newspaper reporter who had covered the Orlando Dexter murder*

How far would you go to protect your land? Would you give your life? On a balmy fall September Saturday, Orlando Dexter, forty-nine, was driving his wagon down the road of his vast Adirondack property when a shot rang out that went through his shoulder and went on to strike and injure his horse. The second shot hit the wooden seat of the buggy and went right through his heart, killing him on the spot. Dexter was only eighty rods from his plush summer cottage. He had gone four miles to Santa Clara to get his mail and was close to returning home when the ambush occurred around 12:45 p.m. A man named Roswell, who worked for Dexter and was following several rods back in his own buggy, found Dexter and alerted authorities.

Orlando Dexter was a very wealthy man who had no friends among the Adirondack folk who lived near his vast property. His regular residence was in Norwalk, Connecticut, yet Dexter was spending more and more time at his summer getaway in order to keep trespassers off his lands. Dexter had purchased the more than six thousand acres fifteen years earlier and built his elegant cottage on the banks of Lake Dexter, which his property completely surrounded. He staunchly refused to allow the locals to hunt, fish, hike or camp on his lands. Some thought he might have been accidentally shot by a hunter. However, local law enforcement and Coroner Mooney arrived within minutes and deemed it an assassination of the land baron because there were two shots and the incident occurred in an area where the hunter would have had to have been hiding in the brush so that he could shoot Dexter from the back. Orlando Dexter's body was shipped the next day to his father, Henry Dexter, in New York City and was accompanied by Orlando Dexter's legal advisor, the honorable John P. Badger. Dexter's assassination caused quite a lot of excitement in Waverly and the surrounding territory, for it was well known that he fearlessly and ruthlessly defended his property and no man, rich or poor, was allowed on it, which caused many people to be upset with the land baron. He even warred with people who owned land adjacent to his. One time, Orlando Dexter was told by a group of men whom he chased off the property that he might end up with a bullet in his head, which caused him to burst out laughing. Henry Dexter was very upset when he received his son's body and immediately put out a $5,000 reward for information leading to the arrest of the killer or killers. Henry Dexter was a member of the New York City Chamber of Commerce and the Museum of Natural History, as well as the founder and president of the American News Company. Henry said that ever since his son had purchased the land, there had been problems with timber men, lumberjacks and hunters who were looking to exploit the rich resources of his son's property. One man whom Orlando Dexter had caught repeatedly on his land had admitted to trespassing 2,928 times. There were even some pending lawsuits about roads some wanted to be run through the property. Orlando Dexter had written a letter to his father days before his death in which he claimed the rhetoric was heightening and that he needed to be steadfast in the protection of his lands.

Orlando was a very educated man, having been a graduate of Harvard, Oxford and Columbia Law School. He had passed the bar but rarely practiced law, instead traveling the globe with his father, who estimated they had done so at least a dozen times. Even those in Orlando Dexter's hometown of Norwalk, where he had a law office, considered him to be a man of mystery who kept to himself, as he was a lifelong bachelor and was always away on travels. People surmised he was a multimillionaire. Orlando had a rather large stock portfolio and was a major stockholder in the New Haven Railroad, among other business ventures. Attorney Badger said no stone would go unturned and no amount of money spared in bringing the assassin to justice. The deputy sheriff of Santa Clara stated that a posse would be gathered to look for the killer, but this never happened, as it was almost impossible to get a single sympathetic citizen. The area was close-knit, and everyone had had a nasty run-in with Orlando Dexter, leading most to say the murder was justified and necessary since he was a very bitter and ornery man who clashed with all the locals. People called Orlando Dexter greedy, selfish and grating. His rich ways and odd mannerisms were a stark contrast to the hardened woodsmen of the territory. The sheriff stated he had suspicions about several people who could have done it, but he didn't have the evidence to push it any further. The deputy sheriff told reporters that the locals were not pleased with the rich people who were grabbing large tracts of Adirondack lands. There were examples listed of landowners who felt wronged by Dexter. Samuel Chambers had owned a sawmill in the area, and Dexter approached him to buy the land. Chambers valued the property at $4,000, but Dexter felt it was overpriced and threatened to place an injunction on the sawmill so Chambers could no longer process timber at the location. Chambers accepted the lower price terms and sold to Dexter. Joe Alfred of Tupper Lake was cutting timber on a plot of land he owned, and when he refused to sell to Dexter at a low price, the millionaire bought all the land that surrounded the lot and Alfred went bankrupt, allowing Dexter to get the land for pennies on the dollar. These were a few of the many stories the locals told about the millionaire lawyer land baron. Orlando Dexter reveled in pissing people off, and the sheriff stated the man must have known his life was in danger, for Dexter's employee, Roswell, followed his employer everywhere the man traveled. Unfortunately, he was too far away to see who had shot Dexter and only heard the report of the gun, with the discharge echoing across the pines.

Henry Dexter quickly grew impatient and raised the reward to $10,000 and asked the sheriff if he could send detectives up to Malone to assist in the investigation. He also asked if hounds could be gathered so a scent could be detected that would lead them to his son's killer. He sent Attorney Badger up north to oversee the proceedings. All was in vain, however, as nobody would talk and nobody would come forward. The entire populace of the area had great hatred for Orlando Dexter, and most were pleased the man had been assassinated.

The case went cold, but five years later, a man from Denver, Colorado, came forward and claimed he knew who did it. Fred Schmidt claimed that he knew the murderer. Schmidt claimed that he was originally from New York at the time of the crime, had worked for the man who committed the murder and was now living under an assumed name out in Denver. He stated that he hid the murder weapon and took $300 from his employer to flee the state. He stated he would only come back to testify if he was granted protection from the murderer, and there was, of course, the matter of the $10,000 reward. The only problem was that when Schmidt was questioned by authorities, his times, dates and locations were completely wrong. When he was questioned further, he revealed he had not been in New York State since 1899, four years before the murder, and only heard about the assassination and the reward from a man in a bar when he lived in Sacramento. Harry Dexter would go to his maker never knowing who had shot his son in cold blood. Some thirty years after the murder, locals still whispered that they all knew who had done it, but the hatred for Orlando Dexter remained strong enough to keep the name from passing from lips to the ears of law enforcement.

Chapter 9

The Grace Brown and Chester Gillette Tragedy

"The evening hour came, the woods that bordered the lake seemed deserted, and at that moment Chester Gillette beat his victim into insensibility. He struck and killed her and then threw her body into the lake."
—*District Attorney Ward*

Nothing says, "Will you marry me?" like a tennis racket to the head. Chester Gillette went on trial for the murder of Grace "Billy" Brown, a crime that sparked national interest, launched a bestselling novel, inspired an award-winning movie and sent a young man to cook in the electric chair.

CHESTER GILLETTE

Chester Gillette was born on August 9, 1883. It all started innocently enough for Chester as a young man of privilege in the late nineteenth century whose family traveled the nation and ran businesses in multiple states. Young Chester was a good student, handsome and had been voted captain of his basketball team at Middle Academy in Oberlin, Ohio; however, fellow students would look back and comment that being made captain distracted Chester from his studies, as he took to working up plays and other captainship responsibilities that made his grades fall. He ended up traveling to Cortland, New York, to work for his uncle, N.H. Gillette, in a skirt-making factory. It was at this factory that young and dashing Chester would make the small-town girls

Chester Gillette. *Courtesy Herkimer County Historical Society.*

swoon with his good looks and manicured mores. Grace "Billy" Brown and her down-home country morals would be no match for his insidious charms.

GRACE "BILLY" BROWN

Born on a farm on March 20, 1886, Grace "Billy" Brown would grow up with the basics in life yet was unable to continue her education past the age of sixteen since she had to pitch in on the Brown family farm in South Otselic. When the young woman visited a relative in Cortland, she became

Grace "Billy" Brown. *Courtesy Herkimer County Historical Society.*

enamored with a city that was small but still had hustle and bustle she never experienced on the farm. She quickly found employment at the Gillette Skirt Factory and was nicknamed "Billy" for her constant singing of her favorite song, "Won't you Come Home Bill Bailey." Grace "Billy" Brown loved to dance and was very thoughtful and cheerful bouncing around Cortland in her slight framed build that topped out at five feet, two inches and one hundred pounds. Grace would meet Chester Gillette and would fall for the handsome young man.

The Crime

Grace "Billy" Brown was in love with Chester Gillette. They made love, and she became pregnant. We don't know if Chester asked her to marry him, but we do know that they took a trip together to the Adirondack Mountains that had been suggested and planned by the young man. The couple took the train and made stops along the way, including at Utica. They took a train up to Tupper Lake and then transfered over to another locomotive that brought them south to Big Moose Lake, where they checked into the Glenmore Hotel. Later on, the conductor thought it strange the man was carrying a suitcase while the pretty young woman had hardly any baggage. The conductor also found it odd that Gillette had a tennis racquet attached to the side of the luggage. Oddities were not missed by the eagle-eyed Adirondack folk, and Chester's mannerisms from the moment he arrived had been considered strange by the Big Moose Lake locals. Chester rented a seventeen-foot rowboat to take an excursion out to the secluded part of the lake.

It was suggested by the prosecution in the trial that Chester hit Grace on the head with his tennis racquet and then dumped her body into the lake. He then rowed ashore, placed his suitcase on the beach, got out and walked the boat into waist-deep water, where he turned it over. Chester testified that his suitcase was dry because they had parked on shore to have a picnic and he had left it there. But the prosecution had the theory that he changed out of his wet clothes on shore and ran for it, jumping a barbed-wire fence before walking down the road toward Eagle Bay. He hid the tennis racquet under a log while he traveled. A group of young men, watching Chester as he silently walked by, thought it strange for a lone man to be walking so quickly. Chester arrived at Eagle Bay and took the steamboat *Uncas* to Inlet at Fourth Lake, where he checked into the Arrowhead Hotel.

In the morning, Grace Brown's body was fished out of the water by a group of concerned citizens thinking the couple had both drowned, not knowing Chester had already made his escape. At the same time Grace was discovered dead, Chester was getting a haircut and then spent another two days canoeing, hiking and talking with the ladies in the hotel, telling them stories of his western adventures. He even asked a few young men if they had heard of the tragedy at Big Moose Lake where a young woman met her demise. When Chester woke up on the morning of the fourteenth, he was met at the front desk by Albert Gross, a friend and co-worker from the Gillette Skirt Factory, and George Ward, the district attorney and undersheriff of Herkimer County. After a short interrogation by Ward, Gillette was placed under arrest for suspicion of murder. Grace's body was taken to the morgue in Frankfort, New York, where the autopsy revealed that Grace was, as the newspapers at the time called it, "in a delicate condition"—what we in modern times would call "pregnant." The autopsy showed the damage to her head from what was believed to have been his tennis racquet. The two were lovers, and it was thought that

Chester Gillette and Grace Brown launched their boat from this boathouse. *Courtesy Herkimer County Historical Society.*

The Grace Brown and Chester Gillette Tragedy

The shoreline of Moose Lake where Chester Gillette landed the boat and fled on foot. *Courtesy Herkimer County Historical Society.*

The spot in the woods where Chester Gillette hid the tennis racquet believed to be the murder weapon. *Courtesy Herkimer County Historical Society.*

Chester didn't want to be tied down to Grace and their child and preferred to be free to court other young ladies in Cortland. The evidence appeared to be circumstantial; however, Chester's odd behavior and running away gave the appearance of a desperate man eager to escape the confines of marriage to a pregnant farmer's daughter. He was taken to the Herkimer County Jail, where he was held on murder charges that, if found guilty, would send the man to his execution via electric chair.

The Trial

The murder trial of Chester Gillette was held in the Herkimer County Courthouse in Herkimer, New York, in the fall of 1906. The trial attracted massive crowds not seen in Herkimer County since the murder trial of Roxalana Druse twenty-five years earlier. There were almost one thousand spectators packed into the courtroom, and many more lingered around outside, anxious for any scrap of news on the happenings. There were dozens of reporters from newspapers from New York City to Syracuse. The tale of the higher-station young man exploiting the lower-station farmer's girl captured the nation's attention, and the media was only too happy to feed its readers the juicy tidbits from the trial of the century.

The 12 men of the jury included the following 9: Herbert T. Dodge, Schuyler; Willet L. Thayer, Russia; Ralph Smyth, Columbia; Webster Kast, Herkimer; Charles L. Edick, German Flatts; Harvey Freeman, Columbia; L.C. Barrigan, Columbia; C.E. Curtis, Ilion; and Marshall Hatch, Columbia. Hatch served as the foreman of the jury. N.H. Gillette was the only relative of Chester in attendance as 150 jury candidates were pared down to the final panel of 12. Justice Irving Rusell Devendorf presided over the case, with District Attorney George Ward conducting the prosecution and Charles D. Thomas and A.M. Mills as the designated defense attorneys. Thomas and Mills asked the judge for a change of venue since they felt that a fair trial could not be held in Herkimer, but their request was denied.

Reporters in attendance who were allowed to go in and see Chester in his cell wrote in their columns that the young murder suspect had slept well and was quietly reading a book in his cell. When the barber arrived to shave the young man, Gillette gently placed his book down and sat in a chair. He would have a clean face for the proceedings. He took great care to look perfect in his clothing. He came across as calm, looking unfazed, unworried, regal and even healthy in his appearance, with one deft reporter stating the young man had even put on a little extra weight. Chester did not look nervous, whether in his cell or in the courtroom. District Attorney George W. Ward, of Dolgeville, had one hundred witnesses from Utica, Cortland, DeRuyter, Big Moose, Eagle Bay and other locations who were all at the ready to testify and place the fate of Chester's life in the hands of the jury. Evidence was felt to be circumstantial by the public and reporters, but the prosecution was steadfast about the strength of what it would bring into the courtroom.

The 1834 Herkimer County Jail where Chester Gillette was held while on trial. *Courtesy Herkimer County Historical Society.*

District Attorney Ward started the testimony with a dramatic telling of a poor young farmer's daughter dragged against her will up to Big Moose Lake by a dangerous lothario who had every intention of murdering the young woman. Grace's parents and sisters were in the courtroom and gently sobbed and wept at the testimony, while Chester sat indifferently, with only a

Chester Gillette's trial was held at the Herkimer County Courthouse in Herkimer. *Courtesy Herkimer County Historical Society.*

slight red blushing of his cheeks. Even when Grace "Billy" Brown's love letters to Chester were read, the young man sat unmoved and unemotional. Ward pointed his finger at Gillette and declared that the young man rowed into a secluded and lonely part of the lake, thinking he would be alone and have no witnesses to the murder; however, a pair of eyes had been in the woods adjacent to the cold waters watching the entire event. Ward called it a brutal, merciless crime where Chester had struck and murdered Grace and dumped her lifeless body into Big Moose Lake. District Attorney Ward mesmerized the packed courtroom with his legalese pontification by stating:

> *Grace Brown, for whom this man is arraigned and charged with murder, was a simple farmer's daughter. She grew up with her sisters as simple farmer's daughters on the family farm and in that vicinity for over a hundred years. A clean, pure girl, of whom no word or breath of scandal had ever been related. She reached an age where she felt she could be of service to her family so she decided to go to Cortland where her married sister lived and to go to work. She went there two years ago and entered the Gillette Skirt Factory where her intelligence and alertness won for her the approbation of all. She would then move into a boarding house where at nineteen years old this young lady would not have the protection of her mother or friends to support her.*

District Attorney Ward painted a portrait of an innocent young woman, fresh off the family farm—pretty, sweet and unaware of the predatory maneuverings of a worldly Chester Gillette. Ward paused for a moment and let the silence and tension build before he launched his spellbinding verbiage toward the twelve men of the jury, the judge and the packed courthouse in downtown Herkimer.

"The history of this man is as important to you, men of the jury, as that of the girl at the time of the meeting of the two. He was born in one of the western states and the impression that he is a boy is no longer true for he is a bearded man with a knowledge of the world and of society and with a sophistication which is equal or even greater than any man on this jury or in this room," declared District Attorney Ward with great delivery. "No boy is this, I say, but a man of mature years and mature mind. In his youth he rumbled about the west. It was upon his travels that he met his uncle, the owner of Gillette Skirt Factory who employed the man. It was in his lowly position at the factory that Chester Gillette had his opportunity to meet the farmer's daughter Grace Brown. It was this man who set upon the sweet young girl filling her with pleasantries and compliments that she took as truths. Little did Grace know he would take the sunshine and turn it into deep shadows."

Ward went on to describe Gillette as a sophisticated and experienced man who preyed upon the innocent Grace Brown, who was naïve in the ways of a lothario. It was pointed out to the jury that Grace had been seduced and had become pregnant by Chester Gillette. He asked her to marry him, but he had the intention of killing her to silence the secret pregnancy. The man felt trapped, yet Grace had told her parents she was to marry the handsome young man. She was in love and had no idea of his plans toward her. When they went out boating on Big Moose Lake, Grace had left her hat on a hook in the room yet Chester had brought along his luggage and his tennis racquet, which witnesses noted was rather unusual for a casual rowboat ride. Once Chester pushed away from the dock and hit that water with his paddles, Grace "Billy" Brown's fate was sealed.

During the trial, District Attorney Ward brought out a huge map of the Adirondacks and hung it near Judge Devendorf. The map had lettering indicating Big Moose Lake and the surrounding area, and reporters mentioned in articles that Chester Gillette had shown great interest in the map and stared at it at great length. Ward went on to call ladies who had worked at the Gillette Skirt Factory to testify that Chester had eagerly pursued Grace while she was tending to her work. Chester's supervisor at the factory also testified that she had asked him to stop coming out on the factory floor to talk with the ladies, especially Grace, whom he had grown fond of, but some of the workers reported seeing Chester walking around Cortland with other ladies. Grace's father testified about the last time he had seen his daughter, but other than that, he didn't have much to lend to the prosecution.

A dramatic scene occurred in the courtroom when District Attorney Ward brought in the boat that Chester had rented and used in the murder. Robert Morrison, the boatman who had rented the boat to the couple and found it overturned in the South Bay part of Big Moose Lake, testified that he saw a man's hat floating on top of the water and a woman's silk cape. When he turned the boat over, it held no occupants, but he did notice some hair caught on some of the screws on the inside of the skiff. He collected the hairs that were now evidence, and some strands were still inside the boat. Some of the jurors climbed into the boat in the courtroom to look at the hair. Ward claimed that Chester had killed Grace with blows to the head with his tennis racquet and, in his haste to throw her over the side, neglected to notice her hair caught on a screw, tearing it right from her scalp. When authorities walked the escape path Chester had taken, they found the hidden tennis racquet. When shown to the jury, the handle had been split from the repeated blows to Grace.

Morrison also testified that he saw pond lilies floating nearby. Chester stated that the reason the boat had capsized was that he was trying to harvest pond lilies. The prosecution proved that the suitcase and the contents were dry, so Chester could not have been truthful in his story. The physicians who performed the autopsy testified that Grace had head trauma, as well as hemorrhages in the brain, that could only have come from heavy and repeated blows from a blunt object. There were five physicians who testified, including the last, Dr. S.S. Richards. They testified that Grace was probably dead before she was dumped into the lake. Modern forensics could easily prove drowning; however, at the beginning of the twentieth century, criminal forensics was in its infancy. The prosecution rested its case after calling over one hundred witnesses.

Chester Gillette was called to the stand to testify on his own behalf by his senior counselor, Charles D. Thomas. Reporters stated that, for the first time, after long hours and much testimony, the indifferent young man seemed to crack

Chester fled Moose Lake by taking Higby Road through the woods to the town of Inlet. *Courtesy Herkimer County Historical Society.*

and seemed nervous, drinking water and stammering a little bit on his words as he retold his tale of coming to his uncle's skirt factory, meeting Grace "Billy" Brown and their Adirondack train trip up to Big Moose Lake. He was gaunt as the stress of the trial had caused the thin man, who had previously been robust, to shed fifteen pounds.

One peculiar aspect of the trial was written up in the November 28, 1906 edition of the *Syracuse Journal*, where it had been reported that District Attorney Ward was trying to prove that Chester Gillette had attempted to poison Grace. A mysterious bottle of medicine had been sent to her home in South Otselic, but she had no clue who it was from. She

Undersheriff Austin B. Klock. *Courtesy Herkimer County Historical Society.*

had consulted Dr. Crum in her hometown and explained that she was taking this medicine for an ailment. The doctor thought she was acting oddly and showing strange symptoms, and when he heard Grace had been murdered, he remembered the mysterious bottle. The prosecution desperately tried to locate the poison, as they theorized the handwriting on the package would match Chester Gillette's. It could not be located. The defense rested, and the entire courtroom waited in great anticipation as the jury met to decide on a verdict.

The Verdict

The case was placed into the hands of the members of the jury, who went into their sequestered room at the courthouse at 5:58 p.m. and asked for their supper to be delivered there, as they were instructed to deliberate until a decision was made on the verdict. After five hours of deliberations and many votes, the jury came to a unanimous decision. They returned with Hatch, the foreman, who read aloud, "We find the defendant guilty as charged in the indictment." With this guilty verdict, Chester Gillette was sentenced to death by electric chair at the Auburn State Prison. Judge Devendorf addressed the convicted young killer, saying, "You have been convicted of murder in the first degree. The sentence of the court is that you be taken by the sheriff of Herkimer County and delivered by him within ten days to the warden of the state prison in Auburn, known as the Auburn Prison, and that you there remain in confinement until the week beginning January 28, when you shall be visited with the penalty of death in the mode and manner and means prescribed by law." Chester attempted to appeal his sentence and received a message from his mother saying, "Have courage and trust in God." There must have been a slight tinge of guilt or fear of being cooked alive in the electric chair in Auburn, as Sheriff Richards revealed that the doomed youth attempted to commit suicide by manipulating a gas line to

The jury in the trial of Chester Gillette. *Courtesy Herkimer County Historical Society.*

a heater near his cell. When he was moved out, the gas leak was discovered and fixed. The theory was that Chester wanted to die from inhaling gas to keep from going into the chair.

THE EXECUTION

Chester Gillette's appeal was denied, and he traveled under police escort via train to the front gates of the Auburn Prison. Chester sat in the prison for almost a year and a half until his dance with the grim reaper was delivered. There would be no governor pardon, as Charles Evans Hughes was a man who believed in strict adherence to law. A commuted sentence would not happen. It was said that Chester confessed his guilt to the ministers who were with him in his cell right before he was executed; however, neither of the clergymen would reveal exactly what Chester had said. On the morning of the execution, Chester was given a new prison uniform, and as he was walked through death row, fellow inmates wished him good luck from behind their curtain-covered cells. The outside of the prison saw many dozens of people, but only the official witnesses would watch the execution. Chester did not look at the witnesses as he was placed in the electric chair. He was strapped in and the power applied almost immediately. Within minutes of having 1,800 volts shot throughout his body, Chester Gillette was declared dead. There was a final statement released from Chester, but it was a typed letter with his signature at the bottom. Some experts believe this letter was dictated by someone else, as it was distinctly different than the young man's other letters. Chester's body was taken to Soule Cemetery in Auburn and privately buried in an unmarked grave. It was an unremarkable end to a remarkable case.

THE AFTERMATH AND FAME

The Chester Gillette murder trial was a national sensation and inspired the bestselling book *An American Tragedy*, by Theodore Dreiser. The author had been fascinated with the trial and kept newspaper articles on it for years until he wrote his novel, published in 1925. His main character was Clyde Griffiths, whose initials of "C.G." were the same as Chester Gillette's. The book was

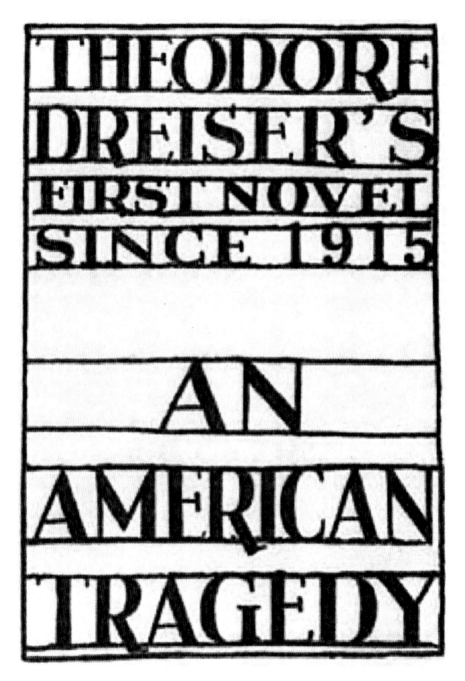

Book cover for *An American Tragedy*, by Theodore Dreiser.

a bestseller and was chosen by critics Lev Grossman and Richard Lacayo in *Time* magazine as one of the one hundred best English-language novels from 1923 to the current age. *An American Tragedy* inspired a play, along with the critically acclaimed and award-winning 1951 movie *A Place in the Sun*. The movie starred Elizabeth Taylor, Montgomery Cliff and Shelley Winters and went on to win six Academy Awards and the first ever Golden Globe for best motion picture drama. A bestselling nonfiction book, *Murder in the Adirondacks, An American Tragedy Revisited*, was written by Craig Brandon. The case still elicits strong feelings from many descendants to this day, especially since Chester was convicted on circumstantial evidence. Regardless, there was no denying that his actions leading up to and after the death were very suspicious. The tragic death of Grace "Billy" Brown at the hands of Chester Gillette remains a criminal case that will forever draw the fascination of the public, with the pure, young farmer's daughter obliterated by the insidious hands of the rich, entitled, handsome Casanova.

Chapter 10
Gangster Dutch Schultz Goes on Trial

"I commit the defendant to the custody of the U.S. Marshall for the trial."
—*Federal Judge Frederick H. Bryant*

WHO WAS DUTCH SCHULTZ?

Arthur Flegenheimer is a name most don't recognize, but the man's criminal alias, "Dutch Schultz," is well known and recognized by mobster enthusiasts and criminal historians. Dutch Shultz had the dubious honor of being the FBI's public enemy number one. He was born in 1902 on the rough and rugged streets of the Bronx and cemented his reputation as a young man with a flashpoint temper who could back it up with his fists. He fought and committed numerous assaults, along with dozens of thefts, yet his street smarts kept him out of detention and jail until he was seventeen, when he was convicted of robbery and sent to a penitentiary for youthful offenders. Never again would Dutch serve time behind bars. For the rest of his life, he would be arrested and indicted many times, yet nothing ever stuck. He came up with his criminal name in tribute to another gangster with the same name and felt it was fiercer than the demure-sounding Arthur Flegenheimer.

Dutch Schultz was a brilliant and motivated criminal, and by the time he was twenty-three years old, he had seized control of number running from his home base in the Bronx. Number running was very popular

New York City "Wanted" poster of Dutch Schultz. *Old Fulton Postcards, fultonhistory.com.*

with gangsters until the lottery was legalized. It was an easy way for gangsters to make big money. His criminal empire spread to Manhattan and Harlem. Dutch used the sale of illegal liquor during Prohibition to boost profits and expand his criminal influence. He brought booze from Canada, through the Adirondacks and down into New York City, where thirsty patrons were willing to pay top prices for high-quality alcohol.

At the time, Dutch picked up a gangland rival in Vincent "Mad Dog" Coll, who had been a criminal associate of Dutch, learned the business and then went into the law-breaking business as a rival. Their war was a bloody and violent affair, including the legend of Dutch waltzing into a police station and offering a large bounty to any policeman who would shoot and

After the death of gangster John Dillinger, Dutch Schultz took over as the FBI's public enemy number one. *Old Fulton Postcards, fultonhistory.com.*

kill Mad Dog. Both sides lost valuable members to the blood feud until a trio of Dutch's gunmen caught Mad Dog in a Manhattan phone booth in 1932. They riddled Mad Dog with a rain of bullets, dropping him dead and ending the war. Prohibition had been repealed in 1933, ending the bootlegging profits for Dutch Schultz, yet he continued to run numbers and spread his criminal power and malfeasance.

THE TRIAL

J. Edgar Hoover, head of the FBI, named Dutch Schultz public enemy number one, supplanting John Dillinger, who ended up dead in a shootout with police and federal authorities. The federal government was increasingly frustrated with the New York City police for not charging Dutch with any crimes and letting him ran rampant over the city. The federal authorities surmised that Dutch was paying off cops, judges, prosecutors and anybody who had the power to come after him. The feds decided to charge Dutch in 1933 with tax evasion based on unpaid taxes on his bootlegging. They hoped the same tactic that ensnared Al Capone would get the Dutchman.

Gangster Dutch Schultz Goes on Trial

It took two more years before Dutch finally turned himself in. The feds knew they couldn't have a trial in New York City, so they decided to go to Syracuse, away from his influence. Dutch was a brilliant strategist and knew what fate awaited him, so he sent his lawyers to the Internal Revenue Service (IRS) and offered a $100,000 payment to settle the matter. The federal government refused. Dutch would go on the public relations offensive and stated that he had tried to pay his taxes, but the federal government refused to take his payment. The Syracuse event ended in a mistrial, with the feds theorizing jury tampering; the public relations campaign had paid off. They decided to take Dutch Schultz to trial one more time, but this time, they moved proceedings to the northwest fringe of the Adirondacks in the small town of Malone, New York. The Malone trial got underway in the summer of 1935 in front of a packed and enthralled courtroom presided over by Judge Frederick H. Bryant. Dutch stayed at the Flanagan Hotel, along with his legal team, until what the press dubbed the "three-ring circus" began. Dutch's team had their hands full, as the press also stated that the prosecution was to be handled by the notoriously fierce and sharp Martin Conboy. Homer Cummings, the attorney general, had handpicked the prosecutor himself. James Noonen, who had defeated the federal and state legal prosecuting team in the first trial in Syracuse, would be back for Dutch Schultz. The affair brought in press from all over the United States that would deliver waves of excitement to the sleepy little town and its hearty Adirondack residents. Franklin County court hosted the legal event that both sides promised would be heated and hard-fought, with neither side allowing a compromise. The "black ledger" was again the focus of the evidence by the United States attorneys, who claimed the book with the numbers proved Dutch Schultz shipped illegal booze across the Canadian border, through the Adirondacks and down to New York City but that he didn't pay taxes on the sales. The ledger fell into the hands of authorities when they raided one of Dutch Schultz's criminal strongholds in the Bronx. Dutch denied that the ledger was his or that it involved anything in regard to his legitimate business life.

The Malone residents commented how the "G-men" were silent and cold when they tried to be cordial, while Dutch's crew was smiling, happy, buying drinks and putting on picnics for the entire town. Dutch himself had arrived in Malone a few weeks before the trial and attended local baseball games, rooting for the home team, going on horseback rides and walking downtown, shaking hands and buying drinks for everyone in the local pub. The government claimed that Dutch Shultz was a beer baron who used influence to keep from facing justice, including the first tax evasion trial, so

Dutch Schultz continues to be a cultural icon to this day and is the focus of the recent book *Dutch Schultz: The Brazen Beer Baron of New York,* by Nate Hendley. Altitude Publishing, June 2005.

Judge Bryant sent Dutch immediately to jail when the trial opened, stating, "I commit the defendant to the custody of the U.S. Marshall for the trial." He wouldn't give Dutch or his defense attorney a reason why, stating, "I will not give my reasons for the order, but if the defendant wishes, I will do so." The defense didn't ask for the reason, but everyone knew it was to keep Dutch from doing what he had done in Syracuse, where it had been theorized the jury had been tampered with. Conboy peppered his opening testimony to the jury, made up of local farmers and laborers, with colorful metaphors with regard to gangland activities and Dutch Schultz's vast criminal empire, spinning tales right out of a pulp fiction dime store novel. Charlie Miller, one of Dutch's henchmen, refused to talk on the stand, though prosecutors assumed he had vast knowledge of the black ledger. The man proved evasive and ended up being jailed for six months on a contempt charge. Schultz himself stated, "I have nothing to fear. I have sweet friends." After two weeks of trial in hot and humid weather, the jury debated Dutch's fate for a day and a half. When reporters cornered him, Dutch was very calm and well spoken, stating, "I'm optimistic over the outcome of the trial. I'll not hide behind the apron of an acquittal. I've made offers to pay and I'll pay even if I'm acquitted. I'll do my duty just as any other citizen would."

The jury turned in a verdict that stunned the feds: not guilty. One jury member told the press the trial was a farce and that the prosecution had nothing on Dutch other than nasty rhetoric. The jury had found Dutch to be quiet and pleasant both in and out of the courtroom. Again, Dutch Schultz used his wit and charm to get out of the tax evasion charge. One jury member even said that Dutch, when he was staying at the Franklin Hotel in Malone, bought many drinks for many locals and created a circus atmosphere, ensnaring many of the locals with his kindness and generosity. It was discovered later on that Dutch had paid a positive public relations team $10,000, and these men went into Malone ahead of time to spread the good word about Dutch and to encourage the locals to enjoy themselves. On top of buying drinks in every local establishment, it was revealed that they had thrown birthday parties for local children. It was also learned after the trial that Dutch had rented out a local dance hall and had invited the entire town to attend, and he paid for all the food and drinks. "Everybody is drinking on me tonight, gents," Dutch said as he addressed everyone at the gathering. Dutch's positive relations campaign was a masterstroke as he had won over the locals, especially when he kept saying he'd offered to pay back taxes and the bloodthirsty feds had rebuffed him.

THE END

Dutch Schultz did not live very long to celebrate his acquittal. While he had been away on his tax trials, his criminal empire weakened, and rivals, like Lucky Luciano and Albert Anastasia, moved in on his territory. It is theorized that what sealed Dutch's fate was his desire to put a hit out on United States attorney Thomas Dewey, which the Mafia Commission denied, as it would have brought unwanted heat to their cause. The hit of Dutch was carried out on October 23, 1935, at the Palace Chop House in Newark, New Jersey, a place where Dutch and his men met regularly, which had made him an easy target. Dutch, two of his bodyguards and his accountant were all gunned down. Dutch languished in the hospital for a day before he perished, but he never revealed who had shot him. His deathbed ramblings were recorded by a stenographer whom local law enforcement authorities had placed at his bedside when they heard he was dying of gunshot wounds. Dutch's last words were incoherent babblings, with nothing to implicate anyone. Dutch went down in history as one of the most colorful gangsters of the golden era of mobsters.

Chapter 11
The Hollywood Golfing Elite Hobnob Accused Robber

"That is Laverne Moore."
—convicted robber Roger Norton pointing at John Montague and confirming the
possible criminal's non-de-plume in court

John "Monty" Montague lived a life most could only dream of in the 1930s. He lived in Hollywood and hobnobbed on the golf course and partied with the most famous movie stars and other rich and powerful people. His fantastic golf game and charming ways made him a natural on the links when he played the best golf courses in Southern California with movie stars W.C. Fields, Bing Crosby, Bob Hope, Stan Laurel and the richest man on the planet, Howard Hughes. Many had declared—Monty himself among them—that he was the best golfer on the planet. Grantland Rice, the acclaimed sportswriter, said of Monty, "He's the greatest golfer on earth." World-class golfer Walter Hagan, who has the third-most major golf victories in a career, behind Tiger Woods and Jack Nicklaus, said Monty was the best golfer he'd ever seen.

Monty was also a very large and powerful man with many feats of strength, including picking up cars so often that he was referred to as the human auto jack. The comedian Oliver Hardy, who weighed close to three hundred pounds, was once in a bar with Monty having drinks and playing around. Monty grabbed Hardy by the jacket and with one arm lifted the robust funnyman into the air and set him on the bar.

Monty's golf bets were legendary and always centered on some kind of trick shot. He bet Bing Crosby he could beat him on a hole without clubs.

"Best golfer in the world" John Montague. *Bettman/Corbis.*

Bing took him up on the bet, so Monty retrieved a baseball bat, a shovel and a rake. They played a par-four hole. Bing used regular clubs and shot a four, making a respectable par, while Monty threw the golf ball into the air and struck it with the baseball bat, sending it 350 yards down the course, where it landed in a sand trap. Then Monty used the shovel to smack the ball out of the sand, landing four feet from the cup. He then got down on the ground and used the handle of the rake like a pool cue and sank the putt for a three,

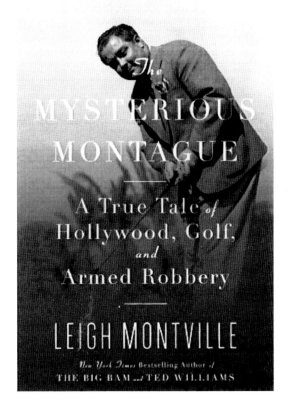

Above: John Montague and comedy legend Oliver Hardy share a meal and laughs. *Courtesy of Ira R. Abrams.*

Right: Media attention carries John Montague into immortality. Book cover of *The Mysterious Montague*, by Leigh Montville. Anchor Publishing, 2009.

which is called a birdie. Bing threw his hands in the air and said, "I've seen enough. I'm going back to the bar."

These kinds of exploits made Monty many friends and admirers in the Hollywood area. But little did his rich and powerful Hollywood friends realize that their golfing pal and best buddy was a wanted man for an armed robbery in the Adirondack Mountains. Not only that, but the man they knew in their elite circle was none other than Laverne Moore, poor man from Syracuse, New York.

John Montague was a suspect in a robbery that happened in August 1930 when the roadhouse establishment Kin Hana's Restaurant, in Jay, New York, was held up at gunpoint by a group of men who came away with $700 in cash. Kin Hana, his wife and daughters were running a respectable family business when men burst in wearing masks and brandishing guns. Kin, his wife and three daughters were bound and gagged, while Kin's wife's father was knocked unconscious by one of the robbers. In the escape, the getaway car crashed, killing John Sherry. The two survivors of the crash, Roger Norton and William Carleton, were captured, pleaded guilty and spent years behind bars.

One man escaped scot free, but a sharp-eyed New York State trooper spotted Monty (whom he knew by his real name, Laverne Moore) in a published photo of a Hollywood event in 1937. The officer got a warrant, and Monty was extradited and brought back to the Essex County Courthouse to prove his innocence. The trial of John "Monty" Montague turned out to be one of the most fantastical in the history of the justice system in the Adirondack blue line. Roger Norton, thirty-five, had been released from prison and was now a truck driver in Cleveland, Ohio. Norton waived extradition to come back and testify against his long-lost friend, promising to "tell the whole story." District Attorney McDonald and two New York State troopers drove out to Cleveland, Ohio, to pick up Norton and bring him back to Essex County Court for the dramatic trial.

When Monty came to Essex County Court, he was arraigned in front of Judge O. Byron Brewster, who set bail at $25,000, which Monty paid in full before he was released for the trial that began in two weeks. In the meantime, Monty went home to be with his mother in Syracuse until the proceedings got underway.

At his arraignment, Monty had to push his way through the massive crowd of people who packed the courtroom. Reporters at the time said that there had not been that many people in the building since the display of the body of abolitionist John Brown. When Monty returned to court, he was

John "Monty" Montague, aka Laverne Moore, at his extradition hearing in Hollywood with his attorney Jerry Geisler. *Tom Sutpen, for the online series "Annals of Crime" #96. tsupen. blogspot.com.*

treated like a hero by the locals, for he was charming and larger than life, and he greeted all the law enforcement officers by name, shook their hands and patted them on the back. Monty accepted a package of mail that had been sent to the jail by admirers from the sheriff, who smiled and said to

Monty, "Would you like to go play a round of golf at the local club?" Monty smiled, winked and replied, "Well, we might go stroll past the course, but you know I'm not interested in golf anymore." Someone shouted out from the audience a question about his future plans, and Monty replied, "My plans are indefinite. I'll be accepting business proposals, but let's get this trial over with first."

The court trial was overseen by Judge Harry E. Owen. Norton was the star witness for the prosecution, with Prosecutor McDonald asking the questions. Norton pointed at Monty and said, "That's Laverne Moore right there." Norton testified that Monty was in on the robbery and was the one who knocked out Uncle Matt with the blackjack. He said the group of robbers, on their escape, had been pulled over by a New York State trooper near Lake Schroon, and Monty sweet-talked the trooper and got them out of the situation. They drove on to Schenectady, where Norton testified that Monty left the car and the other three went onward until the fatal car accident. The prosecution pointed out that Laverne Moore left a set of golf clubs in the trunk of the crashed vehicle. Kin Hana testified that he could not tell who robbed him and could not identify Monty as one of the masked robbers. His daughters Doris, Harriet and Naomi also could not positively identify Monty.

The prosecution rested, and Monty's defense attorney, James Noonan, who at one time had successfully defended famous gangster Dutch Schultz, went right after the character of Norton, pointing out previous convictions. He then read into the record dozens of testimonials from Hollywood friends of Monty like Bing Crosby, Oliver Hardy and others who all praised Monty's upstanding moral character. Noonan then brought Monty's mother, Mary Moore, onto the stand, where she testified that Laverne had been home asleep in his bed the night of the robbery. Monty's two sisters testified and backed up that information. Monty took the stand in his own defense and admitted he used to go by the name of Laverne Moore and even admitted the golf clubs in the trunk of the car were his but denied his involvement in the robbery. He stated on the stand that he had changed his name for he knew he was wanted for the crime and was ashamed to use that name when he was in Hollywood. Monty was calm, at ease and charming and didn't break one bead of sweat as he denied robbing the store or hitting anybody. Many times he got little chuckles from the audience with his witty and lighthearted answers. The jury was handed the case and met in the back chambers for four and a half hours before reaching their verdict. The foreman of the jury rose

The Hollywood Golfing Elite Hobnob Accused Robber

From left to right: John Montague, Babe Ruth, Ty Cobb and Walter Hagen. *Bill Burgess from Bill's Babe Ruth Photos. www.baseball-fever.com.*

and read the statement, "We find the defendant not guilty of first-degree robbery." The courtroom spectators jumped up and cheered loudly until Judge Owen banged his gavel and brought quiet to the proceedings.

A party held in Baldwinsville, New York, to celebrate Monty's acquittal was heavily attended. He claimed that he wanted to go back to Hollywood and was looking to get into the movies, though Monty never got a Hollywood contract and never turned pro in golf. He married Esther Plunkett, a widow with two children, but she passed away in 1947. The rest of Monty's life would be marred with bad luck. He had a heart attack and recovered in 1949 but then was arrested for drunk driving. He languished in obscurity up to his death in 1972, when his sixty-seven-year-old body was ravaged by time. At the time of his death, reporters called him, in reference to his golfing legend, "the phantom of the links" and "the Garbo of golf." He was famous at the time of his trial; however, Monty's body would lay unclaimed in the morgue for over a week until a friend identified his body. The man who at one time was friends with thousands, had charmed the Adirondacks and hobnobbed with the Hollywood elite and putted golf balls with the world's richest man had only a few dozen people show up to pay respects at his funeral. Monty's legacy was one of the most interesting criminal court cases that ever happened within the blue line of the Adirondacks.

Chapter 12
Air Force War Hero Turned Cop Killer

"It's like the walls caving in on you…I've been hit between the eyes with this. I need time to think, to clear the cobwebs and light up the dark corners."
—*Major James Call, when told about the death of Lake Placid police officer Richard Pelkey*

Police officers place their lives on the line every day to protect citizens from the evils of the world, and those who would shoot and kill an officer of the law are amongst the lowest life forms slithering across the sands. It was the shooting death of a Lake Placid policeman that led to a large manhunt in the dense Adirondack Mountain forests for a cop killer who managed to elude capture for 104 days.

On August 5 in the area of Lake Placid, three police officers found a man in a basement of an unoccupied cabin in the woods. The officers were responding to a supposed burglary. The officers surprised the burglar, and a gunfight ensued, wounding all three police officers. Officer Richard Pelkey, thirty-two, died seven days later from his gunshot wounds. The other officers, Sergeant Dominick Valenze and Patrolman J. Bernard Fell, who were seriously wounded, recovered and were able to give a description of the suspect. Investigators also collected fingerprints left by the suspect. Little did the police officers know that the cop-killing burglar was an air force deserter who had left his military position at Barksdale Air Base in Louisiana.

Major James Call, twenty-nine, of Meridian, Mississippi, fled into the Adirondack woods after shooting the police officers and remained on the run while a posse of over one hundred New York State troopers pursued the shooter. Searchers assumed that Major Call was an experienced woodsman, as he eluded a massive manhunt and seemed to virtually disappear. Major Call had flown in over eighteen combat missions during the Korean conflict and had served as a B-47 bomber observer. He had deserted in May 1954 and had been dropped from the rolls of the U.S. Air Force 376th Wing of the 514th Bomber Squadron. It was Major Call's stupidity that eventually led to his capture. He was arrested by Reno, Nevada police for a string of burglaries at "fashionable homes" and told Reno police chief L.B. Gresson that his name was James Chandler Morgan and he had remembered nothing since coming there from St. Louis. A savvy newspaperman covering this case called the Lake Placid police department with a tip that this mysterious robber happened to have in his possession when arrested a newspaper clipping from the Adirondack manhunt for the cop killer. Not only was there the clipping, but Chief Gresson said police investigators also found a wallet in Call's Reno hotel room that had the identification of Elbridge T. Gerry of Old Westbury, New York, a famous polo player whose Nassau County home had been robbed earlier that year. There was also a briefcase in Call's room that was stuffed with stolen identifications from Buffalo, New York, all the way west to Reno. Sergeant Valenze and Patrolman Fell had both given a physical description of Call, and when Superintendent of the New York State Police Albin S. Johnson spoke with Chief Gresson, he thought they had their man. He dispatched two New York State troopers to Reno to question Call and place him under arrest if he was indeed their cop killer. The two officers sent were Captain Harold Muller, who had been supervising the manhunt force, and Sergeant H.E. Blaisdell of the Bureau of Criminal Investigations. They were armed with a warrant to arrest Call and charge him with first-degree murder unless he could prove he wasn't the one who had killed Officer Pelkey. As of the officers flight out to Reno, the manhunt for the cop killer was still ongoing throughout the Adirondacks, especially in Essex County. Meanwhile in Lake Placid, the two officers injured in the gun battle were anxious to see Major James Call in person as they could easily identify their shooter. "I doubt if I could ever forget him," Patrolman J. Bernard Fell told a reporter. "I'm anxious to see this man and identify him," said Sergeant Dominick Valenze. Neither officer had seen photos of Major Call, but they were confident in the powers of their honed police skills of recollection.

When Captain Muller and Sergeant Blaisdell arrived in Reno and went to the police department, they knew they had their man before they even saw Call, as the fingerprints they had collected at the crime scene in Lake Placid matched those of the suspect sitting in the Reno jail. All they had to do was question the man and serve their warrant for first-degree murder. The two troopers were able to return with Major Call as he waived his extradition rights and accompanied the police officers on a flight from Reno to New York City. They then drove him north up to Troop B headquarters in Malone, where Major Call was fingerprinted and then brought to Lake Placid, where he was arraigned. District Attorney Daniel Manning stated, "Speedy action will be taken by my office of the prosecution in this matter." Captain Muller said that Major Call insisted they had the wrong man and would admit nothing, but the trooper said, "This ends the manhunt. We got our killer." The two police officers who had been shot and injured by Major Call said they had seen pictures of Call taken in Reno but wanted to reserve their judgments until they could see him in person in the Essex County Jail and make the identification face-to-face. Police did say that Call showed surprise at hearing he was wanted in the shooting and that a police officer had died from the gunshot wounds. Major Call said at that time, "It's like the walls caving in on you. I've been hit between the eyes with this. I need time to think, to clear the cobwebs and light up the dark corners." Police were also going to question Major Call about a $100,000 jewelry theft that had happened in Lake Placid three days before the Adirondack gunfight.

After further questioning, it was learned that Major Call had stayed in the Adirondacks for over a month while the manhunt was being conducted. Troopers then let the press know that Major James Call had confessed to the crime, although they stated that with the evidence they had, they didn't need a confession. The officers said that Major Call had spoken intelligently and had preferred to discuss philosophy. Police officers said he was being cooperative and was very intelligent and mild-mannered. Reporters stated that when Call arrived, he was well dressed in civilian clothing, wearing a suit, white shirt and meticulous necktie, along with a topcoat. They described Major Call as dark-haired and handsome.

Call was brought to Saranac Lake, where the two surviving gunshot wounded police officers, Sergeant Dominick Valenze and Patrolman J. Bernard Fell, easily picked Call out of a six-man lineup. Afterward, Major James Call signed a police statement admitting to the shooting and killing of a police officer in the Lake Placid burglary. The Essex County Grand Jury was asked to seek a first-degree murder indictment against Major Call. The confession was signed, and Call said he had lost his desire to live after his wife died. Their three-year-old son was taken by the parents of Call's dead wife. Family members stated that Call had become disillusioned and bewildered after the death of his wife, Muriel. Call's

Air Force War Hero Turned Cop Killer

Major James Call stepping off the plane after his extradition, escorted by Captain Muller and Sergeant Blaisdell of the New York State Police. *From* Manhunt for an AWOL Major, *by Leonard Bennett.*

Major James Call was commended for cooperating with law
authorities. *From* Manhunt for an AWOL Major, *by Leonard Bennett.*

mother-in-law noted that her son-in-law was very intelligent and said, "If James is guilty of all the horrible things that have been said about him, it's the result of a shattered mind." Friends from Call's hometown declared that after the death of Muriel, he had never been the same and would sit for hours listening to recordings he had of his wife and lamenting aloud that when he died they would be reunited. Call went on to tell police that he walked south of Lake Placid for three hundred miles and then stole a canoe and paddled down the Hudson River before stealing enough cash along the way to move westward by way of bus, away from the Adirondack manhunt of over one hundred New York State troopers and over five hundred members of the posse.

While awaiting his sentence, Major Call was under close observation, but police said he seemed in good spirits and didn't ask for any special treatment. It was said that he had cereal, bread, butter and coffee for his dinner fare. Major Call went out into the Adirondacks for a nine-hour tour of the crime scene and pointed out all the places he had hid from searchers. Evidence was gathered, and a reenactment of the crime at the cottage was conducted. Call remained calm and cooperative with police as he went over everything with them, including pointing out places of evidence. Within a few months, the Essex County Grand Jury served indictments to Major James Call of first-degree murder, first-degree robbery and petty larceny. Call was arraigned in front of Judge Andrew Ryan of the New York State Supreme Court. Call's attorney, E. Stewart Jones of Troy, pleaded not guilty on Major Call's behalf on all charges. District Attorney Daniel Manning stated he wanted Call to have a fair trial, although Call's signed confession, matching fingerprints and eyewitness identification made what seemed a slam-dunk conviction inevitable. Before the fatal incident, Major Call had burglarized several camps and cottages around the Lake Placid area.

The trial began in April 1955, and Major James Call had his mother-in-law, his sister and his brother-in-law in court to show moral support. A plea deal was made to Call by District Attorney Daniel Manning, who met with Judge Ryan and defense attorney E. Stewart Jones, allowing Call to plead guilty to second-degree murder. Major James Call was sentenced to twenty years at the state prison in Dannemora, a place referred to as the "Siberia" of New York State prisons. District Attorney Manning said that he was convinced that Call would have been found guilty by the jury, but the plea deal was offered because Major Call had cooperated by coming back from Nevada, signing a confession, cooperating on the evidence collection and showing genuine concern and remorse for what he had done. The handsome war hero stood in his perfectly pressed blue suit with his hands clasped in front of his body as he accepted his sentence. The five-hundred-plus-person manhunt was considered the largest and lengthiest in the history of New York State while Call lived off the land and eluded capture. This plea deal brought a close to the case of the war hero turned cop killer. Officer Richard Pelkey lost his life being a hero to the badge while a fallen hero fell down into the hole of madness and murdered a man whose entire life had been dedicated to the protection and service of the citizens of Lake Placid.

Chapter 13
Burn, Baby, Burn

"Forest fire season—nemesis to the conservationist and sportsman."
—*Lithgow Osborne, state conservation commissioner*

FIREBUGS

Forest fires can cause a lot of damage and endanger the lives of people and all sorts of animals and critters. Forest fires can be caused by lightning hitting dried timber and brush or careless campers not extinguishing their campfires, but the most insidious are the firebugs, pyromaniacs who are compelled to start fires on purpose for the psychological thrill. In the fall of 1963, on Hackensack Mountain, near Warrensburg, there was a large forest fire spreading quickly. Forest Ranger Franklin Wheeler led a group of over one hundred volunteers who swarmed up the mountain with water cans strapped to their backs to bravely beat back the infernal blaze that authorities had determined had been caused by a firebug. This latest blaze was another in a rash of fires that had been set on purpose all over the mountain for over a week. Fire burn permits were suspended, as the dry conditions didn't help the brave firefighters whose lives were endangered by the pyromaniac. One of the set fires in the area of Batesville had scorched over fifteen acres of timber, along with three farmhouses that luckily had been abandoned. Another fire in this rash of set outbreaks took the home of Mr. and Mrs. Bailey of Route 28. They had claimed the fire was set by the

Fire tower on Rondaxe Mountain. *Photo by Dennis Webster.*

notorious firebug. Along with these, five other fires had been set in the area of Truesdale Hill Road, where over twenty acres were burned to a crisp. Ranger Raymond Mallory, who was in the Prospect Observation Tower, spotted the latest intentionally set fire and made a call that was responded to by the Conservation Department and the Lake George Fire Department. These two groups combined and did their best but had to pull back as the life-threatening flames licked at their firefighting phalanx. They had to call out and were joined by the North Creek, Bolton and Warrensburg Fire Departments. Sheriff Robert Lilly had determined the fires had been due to arson. Several suspects were questioned.

Natural Causes

Forest rangers will tell you that along with the start of trout season in April comes the start of the forest fire season. Sportsmen, hikers and fishermen who flock to the forest can inadvertently cause fires due to careless campfires, but forest fires can be a result of natural causes. Some forest fires are a result of what authorities call a "perfect storm." In the summer of 1953, a huge fire that consumed one hundred acres of forest and was started by natural cause rampaged in an area fifteen miles south of Saranac Lake. Forest Ranger Fred McLain determined this fire to be the largest in almost forty years.

There was a gigantic storm in November 1950 that felled over one million trees that sat on the floor of the forest and became a dried powder keg timber blanket just waiting for a spark of lightning to ignite it. The resulting fire was massive and threatened lives for many miles. Firefighters had to use spotlights during the day as the smoke and smog blotted out the sun. Hikers and campers had to be told to stay off the mountain and out of the woods as an emergency was declared. The firefighters needed clear trails to maneuver their equipment and didn't want any citizens being burned to death. On top of the dried timber fuel, Mother Nature had provided dry conditions and a persistent wind that fanned the flames and pushed the fire forward. The conservation department and many volunteers had to dig a ring around the fire to keep it contained along with dumping ten thousand tons of water on it. Twelve water pumps and over sixteen thousand feet of fire hose had been deployed in the fire fight. The fire was halted when the winds finally died down and a couple thunderstorms dumped an inch of rain over the area, dampening the forest floor and the dried timber.

A really dry spring also provides optimal conditions for a natural forest fire because the fallen foliage on the forest floor lies on the ground like a fire-ready blanket. The sun's rays can warm up this dried debris, and the fact that leaves have not yet sprung on the trees means no protective shade is provided, thus warming dry tinder that can spontaneously combust.

CAMPFIRE CLUB OF AMERICA

Smokey the Bear has inspired forest safety for generations. *Courtesy USDA Forest Service.*

In New York City's Hotel Astor in the fall of 1911, Gifford Pinchot presented the findings of his investigation of the problems of the Adirondack forest to the Campfire Club of America. Mr. Pinchot spent a good deal of his report on power companies and ownership, but he did talk a little bit about the forest fire problem and the way to alleviate it. He called for responsible and proper logging of the virgin forests, since he had stated that as new young trees grow, old ones die, fall to the forest floor and produce a pile of timber just waiting for a spark that will result in a massive fire that could endanger lives. He stated that logging companies could take out old-growth trees and the result would be a diminished risk of forest fire.

Pinchot stated that preventing forest fires should be the number one task and concern of the forestry department. He theorized that protecting the Adirondack forest from fires was no different than protecting the buildings

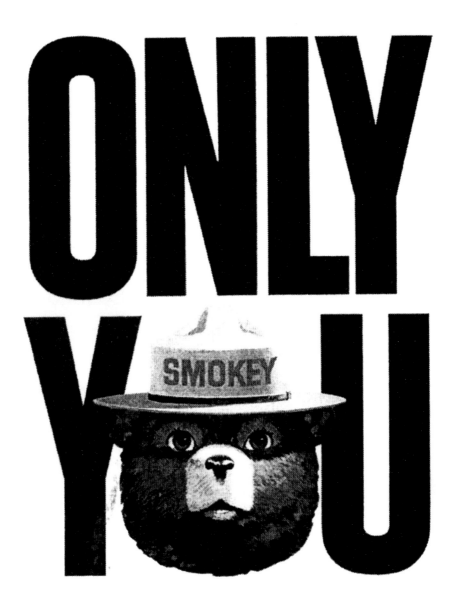

Propaganda poster for Smokey the Bear. *Courtesy USDA Forest Service.*

in New York City. He requested that every town in the blue line have capable men at the ready to attack a forest fire as soon as it was spotted. A quick response can save many acres of forest. He claimed that the cost of fire prevention would be one penny per acre for a tree value of $1,000. He stated that the current staffing of forest rangers was one per 100,000 acres, which was nowhere near enough. Pinchot also stated that burn permits should be limited to only certain times of the year and burns should only happen in the presence of a forest ranger. He also claimed that lopping the tops off trees could reduce forest fires, as they take longer to rot away instead of falling in a mass onto the ground. Pinchot stated that there is disagreement with this methodology, but he recommended it anyway due to his twenty years of logging experience. He also called for a state civil service exam to be given to potential forest authorities who could then be given permanent jobs rather then relying on volunteer watchers who could be unreliable. Regardless of his opinions, Gifford Pinchot came across as a man who loved the Adirondacks and lobbied over one hundred years ago for its protection from potential forest fires.

PREVENTION

Fire tower prevention and education has helped stem the forest fire outbreak. Smokey the Bear, the mascot of the United States Forest Service, made his debut in 1944 with the world-famous slogan, "Only YOU can prevent forest fires." The campaign is still going strong today and is considered one of the most successful in keeping people from being irresponsible when it comes to campfires. Many of the Adirondack Mountains were topped with fire towers that would assist volunteers and forest service employees in keeping a vigilant eye on possible fire outbreaks. Many of the towns that are populated throughout the Adirondacks have dedicated and hardworking volunteer firefighters who bravely put their lives on the line to protect the trees, animals and fellow human beings from the dangers of forest fires. There is nothing that can be done to prevent lightning strikes on dried timber or the occasional insidious firebug and their evil pyromaniac tendencies; however, diligent citizens, forestry agents and volunteer firefighters have stemmed the tide and have kept Adirondack forest fires to a minimum. Smokey is proud of them all.

Chapter 14
Stick 'Em Up!

"The robbers wore masks and fled in a getaway car."
—*witnesses to the robbery of the National Commercial Bank and Trust Company*

The robbers stormed into the National Commercial Bank and Trust Company with one goal in their criminal minds: the theft of cold hard cash. March 22, 1965, was crisp and cool, and the morning business was the usual Adirondack citizens going about cashing their checks, depositing their earnings and applying for loans, when three masked men burst into the bank with the intent to rob. The three masked bank robbers had an accomplice waiting in the getaway car that was running outside as the robbers took all the available cash in the drawers. The customers and employees cowered in fear as Guy Beaudet, thirty-two, of Montreal, Canada, waved his gun around. The lone male teller, Roy Dominy, fifty-three, had enough of the intimidation and threw a heavy tray of index cards at Beaudet, as well as his masked partners Willie DuPuis and Rene Piloh, both in their early thirties and from Canada. Dominy paid for his defiance toward the bank robbers when Guy Beaudet shot the brave teller dead. The price for Dominy's death would be the grand total of $4,900—the total amount of cash that was taken from the robbery. The getaway car running out in front of the bank was driven by Albert J. Couture, thirty-five, a native of Montreal. The robbers fled the scene and made a clean getaway through the northern border and back to their native Canada. The border was only five miles from the bank, yet police roadblocks on the main roadways missed the robbers as they drove across unmarked dirt roads created by loggers.

The robbers were eventually identified by fingerprints found on the abandoned getaway car and by tracing serial numbers off the stolen bills. It would be three weeks until the shooter, Beaudet, was arrested in Montreal, where he swore he would fight extradition to the United States. Beaudet was arraigned before Justice Roger Quinet, accused of being a fugitive on the run from the law. Albert J. Couture took advice from his Canadian lawyer and crossed back over the border to turn himself over to police authorities in Plattsburgh, where he was charged with first-degree murder. The Canadian authorities then put out a warrant for the arrest of the two robbers who were still at large, Willie DuPuis and Rene Piloh. Some of the money that had been stolen was recovered, said District Attorney Thomas R. North, who also stated that material witnesses and New York State troopers had testified as evidence in the murder was collected and was being built toward a trial. Guy Beaudet lost his extradition fight and was delivered in handcuffs across the border to New York State law officers, who placed him in the Clinton County Jail. Albert J. Couture brokered a deal to testify against the other three robbers and was placed in the Essex County Jail, as he asked authorities to be in a different location than Beaudet. He said he'd feel safer because he feared for his life if he had to stay in the same jail location.

It was not long before the Canadian police located and arrested the two fugitives when they surrounded a modest little house in a quiet community just south of Montreal. Just like their bank-robbing, murderous leader, DuPuis and Piloh would fight extradition to the United States. The two appeared before Canadian Justice Peter V. Shorteno, who stated that their evidence for innocence was "flimsy" and said that "there was no room for doubt" that the police authorities from New York State had produced more than enough solid evidence of the men's involvement with the robbery and murder. DuPuis and Piloh were escorted across the border, where they were taken to the Clinton County Jail and placed alongside their ringleader, Beaudet.

The trial for DuPuis, Piloh and Beaudet took place June 6, while Couture was tried separately since he was testifying against the others. The trial took place in Clinton County Court, with Judge James D. Curry from Hamilton County presiding. The trial results proved satisfactory to the family of Roy Dominy and authorities, as all three men were found guilty of first-degree murder. Beaudet, DuPuis and Piloh all received the sentence of life in prison. Judge Curry placed all three men in Clinton State Prison in Dannemore, where they got life with hard labor. For turning state witness and testifying against his fellow bank robbers, Albert J. Couture received a lighter sentence.

Chapter 15
The Adirondack Serial Killer

"I would like to refer to myself as two different persons—Mr. X and Mr. G."
—*Robert Francis Garrow*

The young couple slept spooning together in their sleeping bag under the protective covering of their tent on the edge of the Adirondack Mountains in the town of Wells, when early in the morning, a stocky balding man burst in carrying a .30-caliber rifle. Death was soon to follow at the hands of Robert Francis Garrow, and the resulting manhunt, trial, shocking aftermath and deadly jail escape marked the case of the Adirondack Serial Killer as one of the most tragic, bizarre and downright puzzling cases to occur within the blue lines of the Adirondack Mountains.

CHILDHOOD ABUSE AND BAD BEHAVIOR

Robert Francis Garrow, thirty-seven, testified that he had a very violent and non-loving upbringing in his almshouse childhood home in the Mineville area of Essex County. He claimed under oath at his murder trial that his parents had forced him to slaughter animals at the tender age of eight years old. He testified that his father was a drunkard who once passed out in the street in front of their home, causing his mother to place railroad ties on each side of his father so a car wouldn't come along and run him over.

He also testified that his father had attacked him with a crowbar on the family farm and that he often had sex with the farm animals. He claimed he was lonely and had no friends and was forced to do all the chores on the farm. This was one of the multitude of excuses that Robert Francis Garrow used to justify the rapes and murders he committed. Everyone was to blame but himself.

Garrow went into the air force for a brief stint when he was seventeen years old but got out when he got into trouble with dirty pictures. "It is kind of embarrassing now," he testified in court. Garrow also testified that he once got mad on a job when he was a young man and tore up the place, leading to probation. He then stated that his attorney in that case was a "fairy" and forced him to do things. When he was serving time for rape, Garrow testified that he had oral and anal intercourse with fellow inmates. These events were the precursor to the insidious behaviors that Garrow would eventually accelerate to the crime of murder.

THE CRIMES

When Robert Francis Garrow was twenty-five years old in 1961, he was sentenced to ten to twenty years but would only serve seven years in Auburn State Prison for a rape in Albany of a sixteen-year-old girl. However, it was the murders that would cement him in history as the most notorious serial killer in the Adirondack Mountains. It was a hot July day in 1973 when Garrow, who was then employed as a mechanic and maintenance man at a bakery in Syracuse, came across a young couple camping. Garrow testified in court that he came across Daniel Porter, twenty-two, of Concord, Massachusetts, and Susan Petz, twenty-one, of Stokie, Illinois, asleep in their tent near Wevertown, in Warren County. He stabbed Daniel Porter to death and took Susan Petz hostage. He forced Miss Petz to go with him to Mineville, where he forced her to perform sexual acts, raped her, stabbed her and then threw her body down an abandoned mine shaft.

It was only a few days later that Robert Francis Garrow committed the murder that would end his killing spree and set off years of dramatics, theatrics and humbug antics by the coldblooded killer. Garrow walked into a campsite where Phillip Domblewski, eighteen, of Schenectady, and three companions were camping. He was carrying a loaded .30 level action rifle and had a large hunting knife tucked in his belt. He tied the four to separate

WANTED BY THE NEW YORK STATE POLICE
FOR
MURDER
(WARRANT ISSUED)

ROBERT FRANCIS GARROW, SR.

Description. white - male - 38 - DOB - March 4, 1936 - 5-11½ - 215 - well built - very muscular - brown hair (bald on top) - blue eyes - ("Foster Grant" type) glasses Varied Density "adjust to light" - brown frames - slight speech impediment - tattoo "Mom and Dad" and a heart on left forearm - scar index finger right hand - tip of thumb left hand - large scar (48 stitches) inside left thigh - small scar left eyebrow to bridge of nose - full upper and partial lower dentures - Habit of Always wearing a Hat and Being Clean Shaven) -

When last seen was wearing forest green workpants and medium blue long-sleeved sport shirt. (Aug. 2. 1973.) Residence: 111 Berwyn Avenue, Syracuse, N. Y. - has relatives in Witherbee - Port Henry and Mineville (Essex County) and Schenectady, N. Y.

Has extensive record for Rape and various sex crimes usually involving females under the age of 16 - Burglary - Grand Larceny - Attempted Robbery.   DCI - 566521X - FBI - 121770C

C A U T I O N
SUBJECT IS EXTREMELY DANGEROUS

Is known to be armed with a 30-30 cal. Olin lever-action rifle, unknown quantity of ammunition and a knife of unknown description.

ANY INFORMATION CONTACT: NEW YORK STATE POLICE
Troop B
Westport, New York
Telephone: 518- 546-7611 or 962-8235
873-2111 or 585-6200
or ANY STATE POLICE STATION

"Wanted" poster from the New York State Police. *Murderpedia, murderpedia.org.*

trees and then focused on Domblewski, who displeased him, so he took out his hunting knife and plunged it into the torso of the young man over and over until he was dead. Robert Francis Garrow fled into the thick forest of the Adirondack Mountains. The three remaining teenagers contacted the police and, despite their hysteria, were able to describe Garrow, telling the police that Garrow had told them that he had killed before and he was going to kill again.

THE MANHUNT

At the time that Robert Francis Garrow fled into the woods, police authorities had only sought him in the stabbing death of Phillip Domblewski, as they had yet to discover the bodies of Daniel Porter and Susan Petz. Garrow had left three witnesses alive who described him to police, but the experienced woodsman had a head start on authorities. The police knew Garrow would have to be taken dead if possible since Garrow's sister from Schenectady had told the police that her brother once told her that if police ever came for him again, he would kill himself or they would have to kill him, as he would never go back to prison again, claiming that being behind bars was too tough and lonely. He'd sworn that he'd never go back again, no matter

A New York State trooper questioning motorists at a roadblock in the manhunt for Garrow. *Murderpedia, murderpedia.org*

Over two hundred volunteers joined in the manhunt in the rugged Adirondacks for the killer who was on the run for eleven days. *Murderpedia, murderpedia.org.*

what. Garrow was almost apprehended the first night as he drove sixty miles with a car he had stolen from the campers. He was northeast of the area of Witherbee, where he visited his sister, Mrs. Charles Mandy, whose house was placed under police surveillance, in case he came back. The young sister was charged with harboring and assisting a fugitive from justice and taken to be arraigned in front of Elizabethtown Town Justice Richard Burpee and was held in the Essex County Jail. Robert Francis Garrow took camping gear and a book on camping and outdoor survival from the stolen car, changed into fresh clothes, took a vehicle registered to his name and fled. He came to a roadblock near Speculator and managed to slip through it, but he knew he'd been possibly identified. Assuming the law was hot on his trail, he ditched his car on the side of the road, took his gear and scrambled into the dense woods. The law was in hot pursuit and brought out bloodhounds on his trail, but somehow Garrow avoided capture. Garrow was on the loose in the rugged Adirondack preserve. Authorities assumed that the wanted man had intimate knowledge of the territory and used this to his advantage to live off the land and avoid capture for eleven days, as the volunteers swelled the ranks to over two hundred persons trying to apprehend the murderer.

The next day, New York State troopers were stopping motorists and showing them pictures of Garrow. They had at least two sightings of him, but one turned out to be a hoax. The police flew helicopters low over the territory and had been broadcasting a tape of Garrow's wife, Edith, and their children pleading for him to turn himself in. Later that week, troopers sighted an armed man they assumed was Garrow in the woods and were able to get within one hundred yards before he slipped away. Troopers then found a makeshift lean-to that Garrow had built only sixty yards from Route 8. Authorities theorized that Garrow had used the shelter to observe traffic with the hopes of someone stopping so he could carjack their vehicle. Garrow was nowhere to be found, but there were indications that he had been at the lean-to recently.

It would be terrific police work that eventually led to the capture of Garrow. Troopers were watching David Mandy, sixteen, the son of Garrow's sister. David Mandy had been attempting to deliver fresh supplies to his uncle, unaware that the police were observing. Robert Francis Garrow had circled back to his sister's home. Garrow was desperate for survival supplies; after eleven days, the man was sure to be starving and thirsty. The troopers had a pack of bloodhounds and a greenhorn conservation officer with only eighteen months of experience who would bring the armed and dangerous man down. The bloodhounds had flushed Garrow out, and he was spotted by Conservation Officer Hillary LeBlanc, twenty-seven, of Ballston Spa. LeBlanc ordered the armed Garrow to surrender three times, all of which he ignored, so Garrow ended up being blasted by LeBlanc with four shots from a twelve-gauge shotgun that felled the murderer, who then dragged himself another 150 yards before he had no choice but to surrender. LeBlanc became ill with nervousness in the wake of the shooting. The final showdown happened in the woods near Witherbee, about fifty miles south of Plattsburgh, New York. Robert Francis Garrow was taken to Champlain Valley Physicians Medical Center Hospital in Plattsburgh, where he was listed in guarded condition. Garrow lay in pain in his hospital bed with a fractured right arm and gunshot wounds to the chest and back. Trooper Robert Sanger stood guard outside Garrow's room and said that when asked questions about the murders, Garrow would only close his eyes, wince in pain, turn his head away from law officers and refuse to answer any questions.

THE CHARGES AND THE TRIAL

In the wake of his capture, Robert Francis Garrow was charged by a Syracuse judge with first-degree sodomy, sexual abuse, attempted rape, unlawful imprisonment, possession of a dangerous weapon, criminal impersonation and endangering the welfare of a child. He was also charged with violating federal firearms laws by buying the .30 rifle in a Syracuse sportsmen's shop and neglecting to disclose that he was a convicted felon. On top off all these charges, Garrow was arraigned on murder charges in the stabbing death of Phillip Domblewski. He was questioned about the deaths of Daniel Porter, whose body was found right away, and Susan Petz, whose body wouldn't be discovered for months, yet he refused to answer questions. Authorities didn't have the evidence to charge Garrow with the two additional murders, so they focused instead on the murder that had witnesses. Garrow was taken to the Lake Pleasant Jail, where he awaited his trial and the determination of whether he would be mentally and physically fit to stand trial. It was in this jail where Garrow would lull authorities into thinking he was a mild-mannered, cooperative inmate—until he took opportunity to stab himself. According to Undersheriff Douglas Parker, Garrow was in good shape after the self-inflicted stab wound to the right arm and was now being "very polite."

This was only the beginning of Garrow's attempted manipulation, blame games, grandstanding, dramatics and lawsuits. Hamilton County district attorney William Intemann Jr. was appointed to be the prosecutor of the case and was working on getting a court date to start the trial. A psychiatrist who was appointed by Hamilton County judge George Marthen determined that Robert Francis Garrow was fit to stand trial, but Garrow's defense attorney, Frank Armani, filed a motion in February 1974 that he would use insanity as a defense. Armani claimed he wanted to question the psychiatrist to get a determination on what concluded the non-insanity decision. This move by the defense attorney forced the law to prove Garrow was sane of mind and guilty of murder.

The murder trial of Robert Francis Garrow, scheduled to open on May 8, 1974, would be the first one in Hamilton County in forty-five years, and the jury of 12 citizens had been chosen from over 350 candidates. The choosing of the jury was most uncomfortable, for Garrow was sitting in the courtroom in his wheelchair, staring with his cold eyes over the upper rim of his glasses. During the jury selection process, Garrow asked a New York State trooper to bring him a pillow and prop it behind his back in order to make him more comfortable. The jurors would be sequestered for the entire trial that would be held in Hamilton County Court, Lake Pleasant. If found guilty by reason of insanity, Garrow would be committed to an insane asylum for the rest of his life, or he would be given life in prison if found guilty with no indication that he was mentally unfit.

"I hope the people will keep their minds free, wait and list all the evidence before they reach any conclusions," said Armani, the former assistant district

Garrow under heavy police escort. *From left to right:* Sheriff Deputy John O'Connell; Inlet police officer Richard Payne, pushing Garrow in his wheelchair; Undersheriff Douglas Parker, carrying the handguns; and Sheriff Arthur. *Murderpedia, murderpedia.org.*

attorney from Syracuse. The other court-appointed defense attorney for Garrow was Francis Beige from Syracuse. The three key witnesses were the young adults who were in the campground when Garrow came in, tied them to trees and murdered Phillip Domblewski. The three were David Freeman, twenty, of Schenectady; Nicholas Fiorilla, twenty-one, of Schenectady; and Carol Ann Malinowski, twenty-four, of Amsterdam. The prosecution was handled by District Attorney William Intemann Jr., assisted by Norman Mordue. The three victims testified, but it wasn't until the defense came to the forefront that the courtroom was shocked.

The defense called Robert Francis Garrow as the first witness. Garrow admitted his crime and described how he had stabbed Domblewski to death. He claimed that he came into the campground of the four youths and forced them to tie each other up to separate trees, and Phillip Domblewski tried to grab the knife, so Garrow said, "I went berserk, I guess, or something and I hit him with the knife. And after I hit him with the knife, I tied him to a tree." Under direct examination, Garrow admitted to three other murders. He said

Troopers assist the partially paralyzed and wheelchair-bound Garrow from the Hamilton County Jail. *Murderpedia, murderpedia.org.*

he had killed a guy with his knife who he didn't know that was later identified as Daniel Porter. He also admitted that he abducted Susan Petz for three days and had repeated sexual intercourse with her but stabbed her to death on the third day when she refused to remove her blouse. He tried to recall her name and said, "Could it be Carol?" but when told her name was Susan, he said, "Yeah, okay. It's Carol then." Robert Francis Garrow then testified that he murdered a teenage girl in Syracuse. He had given her a ride into the woods near a cemetery and had sex with her but didn't know her name. "To put it bluntly, she's dead," said Garrow in a cold tone that sent shockwaves throughout the courtroom. The decomposed body of Alicia Hauck, sixteen, of Syracuse, had been found on December 8, 1973, in a wooded section of the Oakwood Cemetery near the Syracuse University campus. The high school sophomore had left home and never returned alive. When testifying, Garrow broke down and cried, forcing a recess.

When court was re-adjourned, Garrow was told that he didn't have to answer every question posed if he would be incriminating himself. He replied, "It really doesn't matter. I'm living on borrowed time." Garrow was rattled in the cross-examination by Intemann when he said he'd plead the fifth amendment. Then Garrow continued to talk about all his crimes but at one point got upset at the prosecutor and stated, "You got me all stirred up now." When asked if he believed in God, Garrow answered, "Very much." The defense called Dr. Franklin Reed of Upstate Medical Center in Syracuse to help prove insanity. He'd had five interviews with Garrow and tried to explain why the man did what he did to Phillip Domblewski. Dr. Reed said Garrow was under an extreme amount of pressure: his father had suffered a stroke and his probation officer had threatened to take his driver's license away. He said Garrow was hearing voices and whispers in his head. Garrow also suffered from terrible headaches and nausea. Dr. Reed damaged Garrow's chances when he testified that Garrow "has lied to me and tried to fake on several occasions." Dr. Reed did tell the judge, however, that Garrow lacked the capacity to understand his crimes. Dr. Reed explained to the packed courtroom that "persons considered anti-social demonstrate the absence of the capacity to appreciate with human qualities that most of us take for granted." He said that within Garrow, "a force sometimes happens that takes over. He can't explain it to you, me or him. It comes from inside himself and is called an ego defect. Garrow sees threats everywhere." Dr. Reed testified that Garrow's sexual feelings led to the killings. "Fear and rage at the mother and father and the sexual impulses got together and were the critical qualities that led to people getting killed." It was discussed in court how Dr. Reed had hooked electrodes to the balding head of Garrow in an attempt to prove epilepsy, but the test had proved Garrow did not have the affliction. When asked whether Garrow knew that killing was wrong, Dr Reed testified, "I do not know." Dr. Reed stated in court that he felt Garrow had latent schizophrenia. Garrow's mother, Marguerite Garrow, testified and said her husband could not testify due to a stroke. Mrs. Garrow affirmed that she had punished Robert when he was a child but never used a strap on her son. She did testify that her husband came home drunk often and once had hit Robert in the mouth. She also testified that Robert had been a bed-wetter as a child. All in all, the prosecution called three psychiatrists and one psychologist, and the defense, in addition to Dr. Reed, called Dr. Jerome Finkelstein of Marcy, New York, as the final person to testify before the defense rested.

The trial had lasted seven weeks and was now sent to the jury. The jury came back with a rejection of insanity and delivered a guilty plea. Garrow was taken away to learn his sentence.

THE SENTENCE

Within days of his guilty verdict, Garrow was sitting in his jail cell in Lake Pleasant, lamenting how "ashamed and embarrassed" he was at the testimony that had come out during the trial. He then went on to predict he would die in prison at the hands of a fellow inmate due to his past sexual assaults. "I can sense it. I know it will happen."

A week after the guilty verdict, Robert Francis Garrow was back in front of Judge George Marthen and was sentenced to twenty-five years to life, to be served at the Clinton State Correctional Facility in Dannemora. Before the sentence, Judge Marthen asked the convicted murderer if he had anything to say. Garrow replied in a voice so low that it was hard to hear it, "No, just that I'm sorry." Garrow's defense attorneys claimed they were going to file an immediate appeal, while prosecutors had to determine if charges for the other confessed murders would proceed. Hamilton County district attorney William Intemann had asked for the maximum penalty and said at the sentencing that he "had committed crimes where he shows no compassion or mercy for people or society should in turn be shown no mercy or compassion." Garrow's defense attorney, Frances Belge, had asked for the minimum penalty of fifteen years to life and said, "We do not have the proper defendants in this court. Garrow's parents should have been tried for failing to care for him." Garrow was sentenced and taken away by heavy police escort in his wheelchair to spend a long time behind bars. But the drama was not yet done.

THE AFTERMATH

Robert Francis Garrow's defense attorneys, Francis Belge and Frank Armani, came under criticism and were reviewed by a grand jury for not revealing the location of the bodies of Daniel Porter and Susan Petz, as they had been told by Garrow where they were. The lawyers had refused to disclose, as they had felt it was attorney-client privilege. The bodies were found, and Garrow admitted to the murders. Garrow later filed a $5 million lawsuit against his defense attorneys for revealing information he thought was private and confidential.

A year after the guilty verdict, Garrow was back in court and pleaded guilty to the murders of his three other victims. However, the most bizarre statement came from Garrow himself, who said in court, "I would like to refer to myself as two different persons—Mr. X and Mr. G. Mr. X has no parents and nobody to show him what was right. I have this turmoil in my mind, this struggle between Mr. X and Mr. G." Garrow said he felt responsible for what he had done and hoped for psychiatric care to "take this Mr. X away from me." In the plea agreement, all the other charges, including rape, were dropped and Garrow was sentenced to three new fifteen-to-life terms. Garrow's court-appointed attorney stood next to the wheelchair-bound convicted murderer and said, "Garrow will be attempting to purge his mind, soul and life of the burden of these acts and will be admitting to himself and all concerned that he needs psychiatric care."

Garrow sat in his wheelchair in jail for years before he filed a lawsuit against the State of New York claiming that he was deteriorating both physically and mentally due to lack of proper medical care. He claimed medical treatment, therapies and supplies were being denied. Garrow claimed he was still suffering from his gunshot wounds, was wheelchair-bound and that prison officials were showing animosity toward him by denying his basic medical needs and comforts. This neglect had caused him to suffer and be subjected to harassment by prison doctors and authorities. Garrow was seeking proper medical care, a motorized wheelchair and a practical nurse to assist him in his daily needs. As a result of his being confined to a wheelchair and his declining medical state, Garrow was transferred to a minimum-security facility in Fishkill, New York, in order to have the paralysis on the left side of his body treated.

THE END

On September 11, 1978, a prison guard at the Fishkill Correctional Facility was making his rounds and discovered an empty wheelchair that belonged to Robert Francis Garrow. The alarms were sounded, and guards and police went on high alert. The supposedly paralyzed and debilitated Garrow had been assisted by other inmates, who used a wooden table leg to pry away the prison bars. Garrow escaped through that portal and then climbed and cleared two fences, one that was eighteen feet in height and one that had razor barbed wire on the top. Corrections and police officers gathered bloodhounds and got on the trail of the escaped killer who had taken a hand-held radio. Police were able to get a scent off the radio that Garrow had dropped as he fled. It would take a few more hours of searching before a scent was trailed and police came across Garrow, who was only thirty feet away from the prison hiding underneath bushes. Garrow opened fire with a vintage ten-shot pistol, hitting and injuring correction officer Dominic Arena in the leg. Officers opened fire and riddled Garrow with several rounds. Robert Francis Garrow was declared dead at the scene. Officials determined that the man had faked his injuries and paralysis in order to wait for his opportunity to exploit and escape. Dominic Arena underwent surgery and recovered from his wounds. It was discovered that Garrow's son had hidden the handgun in the bottom of a bucket of chicken. He had placed the gun in a plastic baggie at the bottom of the chicken bucket, poured gravy over it and then placed the chicken on top. Garrow taped the gun to his leg and got through the frisk from his wheelchair.

With Garrow's death, the exploits and terror of the Adirondack Serial Killer finally came to a close.

Chapter 16
Acid Rain Apocalypse

"When we went up the mountain today, we saw all those dead trees. Something is killing them."
—*John Stock, Adirondack Park Agency commissioner at Tupper Lake*

Human beings are the most powerful animals to ever walk the planet Earth, not based on physical strength but rather mental abilities. Communication, reasoning and opposable thumbs allowed us to rise to the level of gods of the animals, seas and trees. These fall under our protection and usage for our progressive means. Along with our heightened abilities come the aftereffect of our modern folkways—industrialization. Advancements have improved our lives and created comforts like better modes of transportation, enhanced means of cooking a steak, comfortable stylish footwear and power for our appliances. But along with this industrialization and advancement of power plants came a cost—to the trees that cannot speak of their suffering, to the fish that fight the powerful current of the stream and to the environment that is under our protection and stewardship. Since industrialization, humans have improved both our financial situations and our freedom of lifestyle, yet in our rush to advance and improve, we neglected to step back and look at the damage we would be doing to the environment that we are part of. We are not gods that live separate from the animals and foliage; we are a part of Mother Earth, and we damaged her Adirondack Mountain bosom with emissions from factories that mixed residual manufacturing fumes with power plant emissions into our upper atmosphere. The result is highly acidic snow and rain, given the moniker "acid rain," which was determined to be a significant factor in the dying of trees, along with the deadness of mountain waters, mainly in the Adirondack blue line.

Acid Rain

So what exactly is acid rain? It's a combination of air pollution, mainly from Midwestern industry smokestacks and power company emissions that spewed all manners of pollutants into the atmosphere. These pollutants were then picked up by the eastern-moving jet stream that combined with moisture in the clouds to become highly acidic rain and snow, which fell heavily on the eastern areas, especially New York State and Canada. The falling of acid rain killed trees and fish in many ponds, streams and lakes throughout the Adirondack Mountains. It was discovered that acid rain did

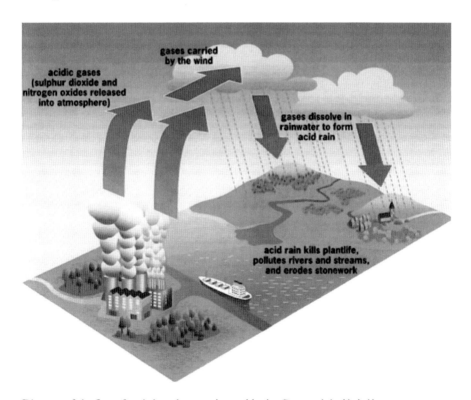

Diagram of the flow of emissions that turn into acid rain. *Courtesy uhohacidrain.blogspot.com.*

not cause damage to areas where the limestone-enhanced soil neutralized the acidity, thus causing no damage, but areas like the Adirondack Mountains, with its bedrock and non-limestone soil, could not counteract or neutralize the damaging effects of the acid rain, and damage was being done to the crown jewel of New York State and America. To be a little more scientific, the Environmental Protection Agency (EPA) determined that acid rain was caused by sulfur dioxide and nitrogen oxides that are released into the atmosphere by coal-burning power plants and factories in the Midwest. These emissions mix with water vapor and are carried with the clouds on easterly winds, and the acid rain is dropped once these clouds hit a high elevation—the Adirondack Mountains.

THE CONFERENCE

The acid rain conference was held at Adirondack Community College in Queensbury, New York, in 1980, and columnist Bill Roden, author of the "Adirondack Sportsman" column, called it an "eye opener." He mentioned that several hundred people were in attendance, including an expert panel, but Mr. Roden was most disturbed by the declarations that further studying needed to be done. This opinion was shared by all except Martin Rivers, director of environmental protection service of Canada, who said the cause had been determined and the time for prevention was at hand. This was after it was announced at the conference that another 50 Adirondack Mountain lakes, ponds, rivers and streams had been added to the original number of 250 contaminated by acid rain and declared dead, with no fish living in the once pristine waters. The scientists at the conference mentioned other damages done by acid rain, like wearing out leather on shoes much quicker, rusting on cars and corrosion of metal on bridges and building infrastructure. Bill Roden stood firm in his opinion that more study was ludicrous since everyone knew where the pollution was coming from, where the acid rain was falling and what damage was being done.

It wasn't until 1995 that the EPA stated that the damage done by acid rain was irreversible and would kill the entire water system in the mountain range by 2040 unless the current Federal Acid Rain Control program was strengthened. The EPA also concluded that, in the United States, the Adirondacks were the most damaged area. It was also determined that "acid shock" was a big reason for the deadening. Acid shock occurs when acid rain

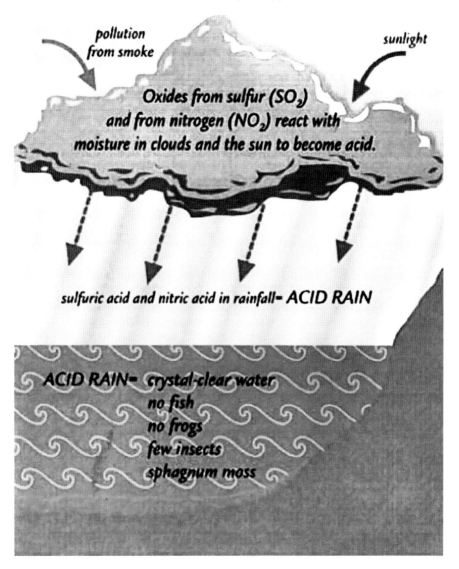

pollution
from smoke

sunlight

Oxides from sulfur (SO₂)
and from nitrogen (NO₂) react with
moisture in clouds and the sun to become acid.

sulfuric acid and nitric acid in rainfall= ACID RAIN

ACID RAIN= crystal-clear water
no fish
no frogs
few insects
sphagnum moss

Easy-to-understand acid rain illustration. *Courtesy www.acidrain123.wikispaces.com.*

comes down as snow. When the large spring melt occurs, the acidic snow that has become meltwater floods into the water system, killing eggs and fry of fish and other aquatic animals, in addition to killing shoots of plants starting their spring growth.

SOLUTIONS

Due to concerned public officials and public outcry, along with media attention brought on by people like Bill Roden in his "Adirondack Sportsman" column, the Clean Air Act Amendment passed in 1990. The acid rain program was set up using this law. Congress mandated the EPA to determine which areas of the country were most sensitive to and suffering most from acid rain and snow and also how much reduction on sulfur and nitrogen dioxide was needed to protect these areas from further damage. The EPA also had to file a report on where specifically these poisonous emissions were to be reduced. In 1992, the EPA created a program that would attempt to reduce sulfur-based air pollution by as much as 50 percent.

GOING FORWARD

The good news is that pollution emissions have been decreased and improvement is being made. There are many that are looking out for the welfare of the Adirondacks, including the Adirondack Council, a private not-for-profit that was founded in 1975 and has thousands of members. It's the largest citizen group protecting the environment in New York State. The group is based in the Adirondack Park and is entrusted with protecting the beauty of the park. As of today, more than 500 lakes and ponds out of the roughly 2,800 in the Adirondacks are too acidic to support plants and wildlife that once lived inside the waters. The Adirondack Council announced on its website (www.adirondackcouncil.org) that the cost to power companies of lowering emissions is less than what Congress had thought when the Clean Air Act Amendment was passed in 1990. There is still more to do, and emissions can be cut further, as damage is still occurring. If you love the grandeur of the Adirondack Mountains, I urge you to visit the Adirondack Council website and educate yourself. The "wicked" in the Adirondacks is more than a serial killer or a timber thief; it can be as simple as water droplets from the sky.

Note: After I wrote this story, an article written by Mary Esch was published in the June 28, 2012 issue of the *Adirondack Daily Enterprise* where it was reported that elevated mercury levels in loons were causing a drop in the population. A loon is a well-known bird that migrates every year to the same Adirondack

Acid rain–damaged trees. *Courtesy www.scienceclarified.com.*

lake in order to give birth to its chicks. These beautiful aquatic birds are known for their haunting calls that echo across still waters. In a ten-year study that looked at mercury levels on forty-four lakes, it was revealed that mercury levels in the sediment, plankton, crayfish and fish of this entire food chain had worked their way up to the loons. The mercury comes from coal-fired power plants in the Midwestern United States. According to the article, the EPA has placed a standard on coal-fired power plants to update their controls on mercury pollutants. We are the stewards of the Adirondacks, and I urge all to advocate and educate themselves on this in order to protect and preserve our most beautiful natural resource. Just because we are gods of the planet doesn't mean we should flex our superiority, for our hubris will be the downfall of the trees and animals under our guidance. It will be mighty lonely when we are alone with our godliness on a barren ball of spinning mud.

Appendix

Maps of the Adirondack Mountains

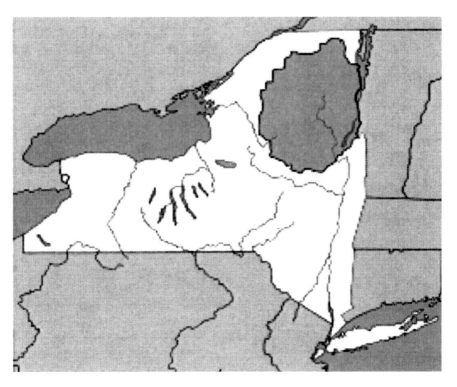

The Adirondack Park is the shaded area in the upper right corner of this map of New York State. The park is massive in size.

ADIRONDACK PARK REGIONS

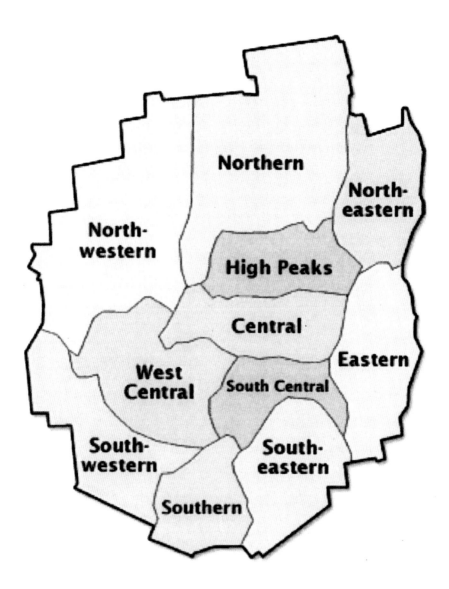

The Adirondack Park broken into regions. *From the Discover the Adirondacks series of books.*

Bibliography

Adirondack Almanack. "John Brown." www.adirondackalmanack.com/category/john-brown.

Adirondack Council. "Acid Rain." www.adirondackcouncil.org/acidraininfo3.html.

Albany Evening Journal. "Sam Pasco Last of Bad Gang in North Woods." May 14, 1918.

———. "Shot from Ambush." June 27, 1910.

Amsterdam Evening Recorder. "Man Held in Reno Believed Missing Placid Cop Killer." November 16, 1954.

———. "Reno Prisoner Placid Slayer." November 17, 1954.

Binghamton Press. "Deserter Call Gets 20 Years." May 7, 1955.

Blanco, Juan Ignacio. "Robert Francis Garrow." Murderpedia. www.murderpedia.org/male.G/g/garrow-robert.htm.

Boonville Herald. "Report Confirms Adirondack Lakes Will Die from Acid Rain by Year 2040." November 15, 1995.

Brandon, Craig. *Murder in the Adirondacks: An American Tragedy Revisited*. Utica, NY: North Country Books, 1986.

Brooklyn Daily Eagle. "Dutch Schultz Jailed at Trial as Tax Dodger." July 23, 1935.

Citizen Observer (Auburn, NY). "Canadian Charged in Killing." April 14, 1965.

———. "Garrow Scheduled to Enter Guilty Pleas." March 7, 1975.

Conway, Matthew J. Highmarket. *As You Were: Two Hundred Years of TUG HILL*. Woodgate, NY: self-published, 1977.

Daily Press (Utica, NY). "Garrow Murder Trial Scheduled to Open Today." May 8, 1974.

———. "Marcy Psychologist Testifies at Trial." June 27, 1974.

———. "No Plans to Query Garrow." December 1, 1973.

———. "Official Says Garrow Had Little Expertise as Woodsman." September 1, 1973.

———. "Probe of Garrow Lawyers Set." August 1, 1974.

———. "Trees Felled by Hundreds in Adirondack Park." October 6, 1972.

———. "2 Women Jurors Seated." May 30, 1974.

———. "Winslow 'Covered' Dexter Murder of 31 Years Ago, Now Recalled Through 'Ad.'" February 13, 1934.

DeRuyter Gleaner. "County & Vicinity News." July 23, 1903.

Esch, Mary. "Loons=Mercury Victims." *Adirondack Daily Enterprise,* June 28, 2012.

Evening Herald. "$5,000 Reward for Dexter's Assassin." September 21, 1903.

———. "Windfall Gang of North Woods Outlaws." October 14, 1899.

Evening Post. "Raids Upon State Forests." October 30, 1905.

Evening Telegram. "Adonis, with Dash of Apollo and Smash of Jack Dempsey, Wanted by State Troopers." May 8, 1921.

———. "Chester Gillette Electrocuted After Confessing Murder of His Sweetheart." March 30, 1908.

———. "Say Gillette Tried Suicide After Verdict." December 1906.

———. "Says Murder of Girl Witnessed." November 17, 1906.

Fairman, Roy B. "The Roaming Reporter." *Syracuse Herald Journal,* 1941.

Finger Lake Times. "Garrow's Escape Still Baffling." September 13, 1978.

———. "Inmates Transferred After Garrow Escape." September 27, 1978.

Fulton County Republican. "Mayfield Man in County Jail." December 27, 1906.

———. "Physicians May Seal Young Gillette's Doom." November 29, 1906.

Gazette and Farmers Journal. "Local Man Is Witness in Moore Trial." October 28, 1937.

Geneva (NY) *Times.* "Believes in Salvation for Grace Brown." April 10, 1908.

———. "Garrow Fears Death in State Prison." June 29, 1974.

———. "Garrow Given 25 Years to Life in Prison." July 2, 1974.

———. "Garrow 'Mumbo Jumbo' on Murder Details." June 19, 1974.

———. "Garrow Shot and Captured, Ending Massive Manhunt." August 10, 1973.

———. "Garrow Silent Under Questioning." August 11, 1973.

———. "Garrow Tells Details of Mystery Murders." June 18, 1974.

———. "Garrow Trial Juror Pool Thinned." May 10, 1974.

Gloversville Daily Leader. "Adirondack Forest Fires." May 21, 1903.

———. "WM. Osborne Dead." September 15, 1902.

Greenwich Journal. "Stagecoach Robbery at North Creek." August 2, 2001.

Independent of Buffalo. "John Brown's Body." 1891.

Journal & Republican. "The O.P. Dexter Murder." November 10, 1903.

Kingston Daily Freeman. "Get Life Terms." August 4, 1966.

———. "Murder Trial in Plattsburgh." June 28, 1966.

Knickerbocker News. "Convicted Killer Seeks New Trial." November 14, 1968.

———. "Conviction Upheld in Bank Robbery Murder." January 8, 1969.

———. "2 More Seized in Slaying." June 16, 1965.

Lake George News. "How to Save the Adirondack Forests." December 2, 1911.

Leader Herald (Gloversville-Johnstown, NY). "Excitement in Hamilton County." June 13, 1899.

———. "Explanation Sought by Garrow." February 22, 1977.

———. "Garrow Attorney to Use Insanity as Defense." February 20, 1974.

———. "Garrow Taken to Dannemora Prison." July 2, 1974.

———. "Garrow to Be Brought Back to Wells for Arraignment Soon as Wounds Are Healed." August 10, 1973.

———. "Hamilton County Burglars." May 27, 1899.

———. "Insanity Defense Pressed in Garrow Trial." June 22, 1974.

———. "I Plead Fifth Amendment Robert Garrow Tells Assistant Prosecutor in Cross-Examination." June 18, 1974.

———. "January Date May Be Set for Garrow Murder Trial." November 30, 1973.

———. "Psychiatrist Testifies Garrow Saw 'Threats Everywhere.'" June 21, 1974.

———. "Robert Garrow Sr. Becomes First Defense Witness in Unexpected Move." June 17, 1974.

———. "Venue Shift Approved for Garrow." August 25, 1975.

Leader Republican. "Desperado Captured." June 21, 1899.

———. "Notorious Visitors." October 8, 1899.

———. "Schedule Speedy Prosecution of Maj. Call on Charge of Killing Lake Placid Officer." November 15, 1954.

———. "Seek First-Degree Murder Indictment Against Call." November 22, 1954.

———. "Troopers 'Certain' Nevada Suspect Is Lake Placid Killer." November 17, 1954.

———. "The Windfall Robber Gang." July 3, 1899.

Lockport Union Sun Journal. "Hollywood's Monty Says He Is Innocent of Robbery Charge." October 26, 1937.

———. "Matt Cobb Unable to Positively Name Monty as Attacker." October 22, 1937.

———. "Montague Acquitted." December 27, 1937.

———. "Montague's Mother Avers He Was Home on Night of Robbery." October 25, 1937.

———. "Monty Acquitted, Plans New Career in Radio and Films." October 27, 1937.

———. "Norton Testifies Monty Took Part of Holdup at Jay." October 21, 1937.

———. "Norton to Testify Against Monty." September 7, 1937.

———. "This Week in New York State." October 23, 1937.

Marullo, Fr. Lawrence. *St. Mary's Catholic Church History*. Constableville, NY: self-published, 2006.

Messenger. "Golf by Bob Ditch." February 14, 1979.

New Jersey History's Mysteries. "The Dying Dutchman." www.njhm.com/dutchschultz.htm.

New York Daily Tribune. "Dexter to Increase Reward." September 23, 1903.

———. "O.P. Dexter Shot Dead." September 20, 1903.

New York Herald. "Adirondack Forest Will Soon Disappear." May 14, 1891.

New York History Net. "John Brown's Farm." www.nyhistory.com/gerritsmith/nelba.htm.

New York Post. "Policy Gang in 1935 Went Free by Mere Walkout on Court." July 22, 1937.

New York State Adirondack Park Agency. "About New York State Park Agency." http://apa.ny.gov/about_agency/index.html.

New York State Department of Environmental Conservation. "Environmental Impact of Acid Deposition: Lakes." www.dec.ny.gov/chemical/8631.html.

New York Times. "Bought by the Central." August 9, 1892.

———. "Railroad Rivalry in the Adirondacks." September 14, 1902.

———. "Two Highwaymen Rob an Adirondack Coach." August 15, 1901.

Niagara Falls (NY) Gazette. "Call Takes Tour of Murder Scene with Troopers." November 23, 1954.

———. "Murder Case Extradition Lost." August 25, 1965.

———. "Rampaging Adirondack Fire Ringed in by Huge Firelane." July 20, 1953.

North News. "Bank Killers' Trial Set for June 6." April 4, 1966.

Oswego Palladium-Times. "Call Pleads Innocent to Indictments." January 15, 1955.

———. "A Strange Case." September 25, 1903.

Oswego Valley News. "Lack of Information Hampers Battle Against Acid Rain." July 23, 1981.

Otsego Farmer. "Local Brevities." June 8, 1945.

Poughkeepsie Eagle News. "Schultz Loses His Freedom." July 24, 1935.

Rochester Democrat & Chronicle. "Forest Fires Open Earlier in This State." March 8, 1937.

Roden, Bill. "Information Forum on Acid Rain." *Adirondack Sportsman,* July 1980.

Roman Citizen. "Lone Highwayman Was Bold." August 15, 1901.

Schenectady Gazette. "Call Flown East, Leaves Today for Lake Placid." November 20, 1954.

St. Lawrence Herald. "Murder of Orlando Dexter." September 25, 1903.

Syracuse American. "Eve of Schultz Trial Finds Both Sides Determined." July 21, 1935.

———. "Never Beer Baron, Not Rich, Asserts Dutch Schultz." December 22, 1934.

Syracuse Herald. "Sam Pasco Arraigned." July 15, 1903.

———. "State to Improve John Brown's Home." Sunday, May 14, 1911.

Syracuse Journal. "Father of Grace Brown on Stand." November 19, 1906.

———. "Gillette on Stand Tells His Story." November 28, 1906.

———. "Gillette's Battle for Life Begins." November 12, 1906.

———. "Gruesome Evidence in Skiff Gillette Hired." November 23, 1906.

———. "Package of Poison Was Sent to Grace Brown." November 28, 1906.

———. "Schultz Henchman Jailed for 6 Months on Contempt Charge." July 30, 1933.

———. "Tightly Woven Web May Prove Gillette Guilty." November 28, 1906.

Taylor, Sister Mary Christine. *Eras of Fourteen Bishops, Diocese of Ogdensburg.* http://www.dioogdensburg.org/About/History/1872tr1962.pdf.

Tonowanda News. "Accused Killer Awaits Action by Grand Jury." November 22, 1954.

———. "Convicted Murderer Loses Appeal for a New Trial." December 31, 1968.

———. "Fishkill Escapee Is Shot Dead Near Prison." September 12, 1978.

———. "The York State Story." April 23, 1955.

Warrensburgh News. "Forest Fires Are Reported." May 4, 1922.

———. "Forest Fires Plague Adirondacks, Blame Firebug in Batesville Blaze." October 10, 1963.

Watertown Daily Times. "County and Neighboring: The Windfall Gang." October 20, 1899.

———. "Gangster Dutch Schultz Was Slain Soon After Controversial North Trial." January 11, 1968.

———. "Garrow Memory Lapses Target of Prosecution in Murder Trial." June 24, 1974.

———. "Gillette Put to Death in Electric Chair." March 30, 1908.

———. "Judge's Ruling on Getaway Car Allows Retrial for Bank Robber." June 1, 1973.

———. "Man to Get New Trial in Murder." March 31, 1968.

———. "Mystery Man, Termed 'Greatest Golfer Ever,' Dies in Hollywood at 67." May 27, 1972.

———. "Says He Knows Who Killed O.P. Dexter." November 6, 1908.

———. "Second Man Arrested in North Bank Robbery." April 14, 1965.

Wikipedia. "Adirondack Mountains." http://en.wikipedia.org/wiki/Adirondack_Mountains.

The World. "Broke Jail to Be Killed." June 13, 1899.

About the Author

Dennis Webster is the author of *Wicked Mohawk Valley* and *Haunted Mohawk Valley* and editor, compiler and story contributor to *Adirondack Mysteries*, volumes 1 and 2, as well as the fiction novel *Daisy Daring & the Quest for the Loomis Gang Gold*. He's a paranormal investigator with the Ghost Seekers of Central New York. He lives in the foothills of the Adirondack Mountains with his family and his howling beagle. He can be reached at denniswbstr@gmail.com.